The Prime Minister's Potato

Anne-Marie Condé

Anne-Marie Condé is a curator and historian living in Canberra. Her published work mainly concerns the history of archives, recordkeeping and museums in Australia.

Anne-Marie Condé

The Prime Minister's Potato

and other essays

First published in Australia in 2025
by Upswell Publishing
Perth, Western Australia
upswellpublishing.com

Upswell operates in the city of Perth, on ancient country of the Whadjuk people of the Noongar nation who remain the spiritual and cultural custodians of this beautiful land. We acknowledge their continuing connection to country and express gratitude to elders past and present for their strength and creativity...Always was, always will be, Aboriginal land.

This book is copyright. Apart from any fair dealing for the purpose of private study, research, criticism or review, as permitted under the *Copyright Act 1968*, no part may be reproduced by any process without written permission. Enquiries should be made to the publisher.

Copyright © 2025 Anne-Marie Condé

The moral right of the author has been asserted.

ISBN: 978-1-7637331-3-8

 A catalogue record for this book is available from the National Library of Australia

Cover image: Edward Condé
Cover design by Chil3, Fremantle
Typeset in Foundry Origin by Lasertype
Printed by Lightning Source

Upswell Publishing is assisted by the State of Western Australia through its funding program for arts and culture.

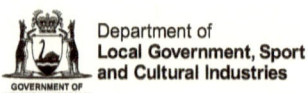

For my parents, brothers and sons

Contents

The Making of a Miniaturist	9
My Brother Clive	19
The Telegram	35
The Names Inlaid	45
Unquiet Stories from Liffey	55
Rock, Water, Paper	67
What Did *You* Do in the War, Sandy?	77
From a Distance	87
Arthur Stace's Single Mighty Word	95
Afternoon Tea with Mary Gilmore	107
Lifting the Shadow	119
Memories, $2 Each	129
You're Not Going to *Buy* It, Are You?	139
Charles Darwin, George Frankland and Me	147
A Rainy Day in Hobart	161
Ben Chifley's Pipe	169
John Curtin's Potato	177
Further Reading	185
Acknowledgements	191

The Making of a Miniaturist

This book emerges from thirty years of working with the stuff of history. I am a historian and a museum curator, and as a curator I am always interested in *things*. It's my job to research the history and significance of objects, photographs and textual records. And because I am a curator and work within institutions – museums and archives – my working life has been spent with a well-established set of procedures and protocols for acquiring and interpreting objects.

Quite often in recent years I've become restless. During these times I think of the Mole in Kenneth Grahame's *The Wind in the Willows*. When the book opens we discover the Mole hard at work with duster, brush and pail, spring-cleaning his little underground house. Presently he is overcome by the thought of spring with "its spirit of divine discontent and longing". I know how that feels. Like the Mole, I sometimes fling aside my databases and spreadsheets and emails ("Bother!" he exclaims. And "O blow!") and bolt for the door. Out in the sunlight, so to speak, in the warm grassy meadow, I give myself the freedom to play about with whatever little pieces of history catch my fancy. I write about them and hope that they will take the fancy of a reader as well. I don't mess about in boats like the Mole and his friend the Water Rat (I hate boats), although I do appreciate the charming idleness of it. Instead, I mess about in history.

What catches my attention are stories and memories outside the museum walls. In the essays in this book, I stumble through the long grass in a remote cemetery in Tasmania, return to my old school, go shopping in collectables shops, and pause to wonder why someone would send a *potato* as a gift to a prime minister. Anyone can enrich – or challenge – themselves by noticing the world around them and asking questions about how it came to be as it is. There is as much history to be discovered in a row of trees or a row of old shops as in a row of books.

Friends sometimes ask what is the thread or purpose that connects the essays I write, and, embarrassingly, I never have much of an answer. I just amble about, noticing this, picking up that, allowing myself to become wholly engrossed in something for no reason, like a child examining a spider's web or a shiny pebble. Obscure lives are the ones I like best; the more obscure the better. Each essay is framed entirely by my way of seeing, but this book is not a memoir. Neither is it a conventional work of history nor, still less, a manual for curators. I'm not writing for experts. If anything – and this is the only connecting thread I can think of – it is a series of meditations on how the past can be understood through the interactions of people, places and things.

* * *

My own sense of the past began when, as a small child, I would pore over my parents' wedding album. Turning its creaky pages, I'd ask my mother all sorts of questions about where the wedding had taken place (Brisbane), who made her dress (she did), and who all the guests were. I would peer hard at the photographs to find myself in them because I couldn't accept Mum's smiling explanation that I had not "arrived" yet. I looked and looked, especially at a particular photograph taken in the church, certain that a little round smudge here or there among the guests must have been my little baby head. I remember insisting almost tearfully that I *must* have been there. There was Mum and there was Dad, so where was *I*?

These are questions every child asks. Where did I come from? Where do I belong? In every culture there are explanations in story and song to help children orientate themselves in place and time. These stories will begin within the child's family, and in the Western culture in which I grew up, the wedding album can be a storybook right there about the family and community into which the child was born.

That wedding album was the first artefact marking the development of my own historical consciousness. My second such encounter occurred at school, although not through any formal classroom teaching. I received all my schooling at Mount Carmel College, a Catholic school for girls in the affluent Hobart suburb of Sandy Bay. I was a solitary child and spent a lot of time wandering in remote parts of the school, often noticing odd bits of broken blue-and-white china in the soil. I always pounced on these, dusting them off with my fingers and slipping them into my tunic pocket. At home I kept my finds in a shoebox in my bedroom. I would clean them up some more and play about trying to piece them together. I was thrilled when I occasionally found two or three pieces that belonged. The heaviness of some of them makes me think now that they must have been from meat dishes or soup tureens, but as a child I wouldn't have known what those were. Mum served our dinner in the kitchen directly onto dinner plates and bowls.

The other puzzle was that these broken bits seemed to have nothing to do with the current life of the school. Teachers in the staffroom never ate off blue-and-white china. So how on earth did they get there? Clearly this place had once been something else. The heart of the school was an old single-storey house which in my time contained offices and classrooms (and a tiny school library, my favourite place), but evidently it was much older than the rest of the school. Even as a very young child I knew it was beautiful. I loved how it sat serenely indifferent to the hubbub of school life. I loved its mellow sandstone, its bay windows and deep veranda overlooking the River Derwent. But we were told never to run on the veranda lest we bring the old structure down, and indeed the veranda was removed at some stage while I was still in primary school. Without it the house always looked naked to me, but I still loved it. There was nothing beautiful about the

1950s suburb I lived in. (Not Sandy Bay – no way could my parents have afforded that.)

Mount Carmel occupied (and still occupies) a large block from Sandy Bay Road at the front up to Quorn Street at the rear, and over many years newer buildings have been added to accommodate the school. Long before I started in 1970, the old house had been extended at the back in liverish red brick, deeply unsympathetic to the golden sandstone of the original structure. Most of the other school buildings, plain and practical, had been plonked down in the 1960s. The contrast between old and new was impossible to miss and it was this, I think, that fastened my interest on the history of the place. Nothing that was new was pleasant to look at.

I somehow learned that Mount Carmel's original school building had once been a family home, and the rough stone building behind it (since demolished), which we used as an assembly hall and later an art room, had been the stables. But no-one told me anything about who had lived there, and no-one except me seemed in the least interested. In thirteen years I learned nothing about the history of this place. I was perplexed and saddened to think that the people who had once lived there had been so quickly forgotten. Looking back, I can see that I was too young, really, to be already haunted by the past, but that is how I became fascinated by the lives of ordinary people. That is why, as a historian, I have always been drawn to the local and the domestic, the intimate and the intricate. Mount Carmel made me a miniaturist.

As a young adult I had plenty of other things to think about, so when I realised that my mother had turfed my collection of old china after I left home, I was only mildly regretful. Years later – just recently in fact, in a bout of Covid-induced introversion – I harked back to own past and thought again about that shoebox full of china fragments. What *was* that all about? Surely in these days of the internet, I thought, there should be *something* I could fossick out about the history of that place? A few minutes on the school website, where at last there is a little historical section, finally gave me the one piece of information that I had never had, but which unlocked the history: Lauramont.

This was the name of the property before it became a school. I'd never heard it before; in my time, no-one ever spoke of Lauramont. But it was all I needed to solve the mysteries of my school days.

* * *

Here is what I found. Lauramont was part of the holdings of the Lord family. Ex-convict James Lord began purchasing land in the area now called Sandy Bay in 1817, and he and his son David eventually owned several farms in the district, which were run as businesses by hired managers. Pastoralist, banker and trader: David Lord built on his father's success and in 1827 was considered so wealthy that he "knew not the extent of his own riches", although it was also said that both father and son had amassed their fortunes by dishonest as well as honest means. Lauramont eventually passed to David's grandson Octavius Lord, born in 1855. Included in his inheritance was the present site of the University of Tasmania and large tracts of land on Mount Nelson, rising 318 metres behind Sandy Bay.

Sources differ as to whether Octavius or his father built the house, and I can't discover anything about the "Laura" in Lauramont. The house, beautifully sited above Sandy Bay Road (or High Street, as it was known originally), was not large: about eight rooms plus outbuildings. It was surrounded by land now bound by present-day Sandy Bay Road, Earl Street, Quorn Street and Nelson Road. In 1888 Octavius married Ida Watchorn, daughter of a prominent business and legal family in Hobart, and the couple had three sons, Clive (born 1889), Darrell (1894) and Athol (1897). Octavius didn't farm the land but instead pursued a career as an accountant at Hobart's General Post Office. The family was comfortably off and, with Ida as hostess, Lauramont became the centre of many entertainments for Hobart's upper crust, especially in the decade or so before the First World War.

"Mrs Octavius Lord's" dinners and parties were often noted in the local and interstate press. For instance, the "prettiest girls" were seen at a "small dance" for visiting naval officers in 1907. At a party in 1909,

Octavius Lord, 1895
Libraries Tasmania NS738-1-1546

guests were received in the garden and, "under a canopy of beautiful walnut trees", enjoyed strawberries and cream and other delicacies. For an evening dance in 1910, the drawing room was lit with dozens of candles which, it was said, threw a much "softer and prettier light" than gas or electricity would have. Raspberries and cream were served on the veranda at an "at home" at Lauramont in 1915, and the rooms were decorated with roses, carnations and sweet peas. That veranda looked across the garden to the river and there were far fewer houses then. No noisy schoolgirls, no grumpy school secretaries, no squashed bananas in schoolbags, and no rancid school milk.

Octavius was a keen gardener known for his prize-winning blooms, so the flowers, berries and walnuts were probably his work. Some of the walnut trees survived into old age and were still there in the 1970s when I was in primary school. We used to wait until the fruit had fallen, strip off the green husks, stamp the shells open and eat the nuts. They were bitter and not very palatable, but that didn't matter. I intuited that the tree had been there longer than the school, and that pleased me.

A photograph taken in 1910 from Dunkley's Point, where Wrest Point Casino is now, gives a view of across the water towards Lauramont; the bi-coloured veranda can be seen faintly in the very centre of the image. Ida Lord was enjoying the height of her social success then, but newer houses had begun springing up. How I would have loved to have seen this photograph when I was a youngster.

The Lords' days as Sandy Bay's self-appointed landed gentry couldn't last. The war didn't seem to affect them directly (none of their sons enlisted), but creeping suburbia got to them instead. Sandy Bay was turning into a most desirable riverside suburb and the Lords were perfectly positioned to turn a handsome profit. Octavius first began subdividing parcels for sale in the 1890s, and in 1909 he offered forty more blocks. He retired in 1913 owing to ill-health, after thirty-nine years' service with the Postmaster-General's Department, and died in 1927 aged seventy-one. Immediately, more of the estate was sold, including a block on Sandy Bay Road which had been part of the Lauramont garden.

The last of the Lauramont estate – the original house plus outbuildings and two acres of land – was sold in 1935, by which time it was surrounded by small suburban blocks. It was bought initially by two teachers who converted it into a girls' private school known as the Fahan School, but the site was too small for them, and in 1944 they sold it to the Catholic archdiocese of Hobart and moved Fahan to a much larger site in lower Sandy Bay. From 1947 the Sisters of Charity operated the school as Mount Carmel School.

As to the question of why those shards of crockery ended up in the soil, the answer is simple. I learned from online discussions among gardeners, especially people with plots which had been cultivated a long time, that there are a few explanations. One is that before the days of municipal rubbish collection, people used to bury any rubbish they could not burn or otherwise dispose of. Cups and plates broken beyond repair aren't good for much, so out they'd go. However, in that case, I would also expect to find broken bottles, or old shoes perhaps, and I never did. The more plausible possibility is that because china is full of bone ash, and therefore contains nitrogen and phosphorus, it was used to break up the soil and act as a natural fertiliser. This is the kind of thing Octavius might have done. I can easily imagine him in his old gardening clothes, scooping up the broken crocks set aside for him in the kitchen and carrying them out to his vegetable and flower beds.

Sandy Bay with Mount Wellington behind, 1910
Photographer: James Chandler
Libraries Tasmania NS869-1-362

I never thought to record exactly where in the school grounds I found the most fragments but if they been clustered, that would have been a clue. A career as an archaeologist was obviously not in my future.

* * *

When I think of Lauramont's heyday, I imagine the children who were there before me: three boys with grubby knees, climbing trees to hurl walnuts at each other while they watched the boats passing by on the Derwent. Clive, Darrell and Athol Lord all lived their entire lives in Sandy Bay and had houses on blocks subdivided from Lauramont. Darrell became a businessman and lived around the corner in Nelson Road. He died in 1949. Athol took up dairy farming and in 1921 purchased land in lower Sandy Bay. He subdivided and sold it in 1941, and at the time of his death in 1979 was living in David Avenue, up the slope a little from Lauramont. In his final years he would have heard the merry shrieks of schoolgirls every day; I might even have passed him in the street sometimes. The oldest son, Clive, had a remarkable life, and it is here that the story of the Lords of Lauramont starts to unravel.

I had a lovely time in that first Covid year returning to my schoolgirl dreams of parties and dances in flower-filled rooms, in which young ladies and gentlemen ate strawberries and cream off the very same blue-and-white china I'd later found, broken and forgotten. I was amazed that my discoveries were so close to what I had imagined. Gradually, however, I became more and more engrossed in the life of Clive Lord, and that demanded a consideration of the ethical responsibilities that go with the study of history. Around this time I happened upon a remark by art historian John Berger that sums it up nicely: "The past is not for living in; it is a well of conclusions from which we draw in order to act." I knew then that the time had come to pack away the dress-up box.

What I did next – how I acted – is explained in the next essay.

My Brother Clive

It's an odd thing to discover a sense of fellowship with a deceased stranger. I never met Clive Lord. He died in 1933, and I only learned about him by chance, in 2020, in the empty, hours gifted me by the Covid pandemic. Searching for distraction, I dug deep into this man's life story, drawn to him by the things we have in common. We both were born and grew up in Hobart, and his childhood home in Sandy Bay, known as Lauramont, was eventually sold and turned into a Catholic school. Much later I attended that school, Mount Carmel College, for thirteen years and it became as familiar to me as my own home.

After university I moved to the mainland, as many young Tasmanians do. But Clive Lord made a career for himself in Hobart and, as it turned out, never needed to move away from home at all. In about 1915, when he was ready to marry, his father Octavius Lord ceded one of the blocks of the Lauramont estate to him, on which to build a house of his own. By then, the farms and other large holdings in this area of Hobart were being sold off for suburban development, and grids of streets laid out. Clive established a substantial house and garden at 5 Quorn Street, at the rear of his childhood home. He married a Sydney-born woman, Doris Mills, and took her to Quorn Street to live.

Decades on, our school bus used to drop off and pick up outside this house, and as a schoolgirl I must have glanced at it hundreds of times without paying much attention. It was a melancholy place, I thought, built in dark red brick, rather secretive, half-hidden as it was from the street by hedges and shrubs. The house next to it at 7 Quorn Street was much more familiar to me because it had been bought for the school and converted into a convent for the nuns. This was a pretty house with a latticed porch, and beds of roses in front of its diamond-paned windows.

I knew nothing of Clive Lord then, but now realise he packed many achievements into his short life. He deserves to be better known, although a full biography would be hampered by the fact that few, if any, personal papers appear to have survived. Even so, I feel a strong emotional association with him. I already have two brothers, but at times Clive feels like an extra brother I didn't know I had, an adoptee perhaps, someone whose life feels curiously similar but simultaneously divergent to my own. What follows is an account of how I grappled with this intimacy and distance.

* * *

As a young man Clive Lord established himself as an architect, but it was the outdoors that really drew him. In 1917 he scored a position at the Tasmanian Museum and Art Gallery and in 1923 he was made director. As his career flourished he became known as a scientist, an explorer, a writer of lyrical prose about Tasmania's wilderness, and an energetic advocate for the protection of Tasmanian flora, fauna and historic sites.

Lord designed his own house and in 1916 published an account of how he went about it in the architects' journal *Building*. The house was situated, he wrote, on a rising knoll giving "unlimited views of mountain, hill and river". The main rooms were lined with redwood and Tasmanian hardwood, as well as cedar he had obtained from a demolished church. The largest windows were at the back of the house, facing east, to take advantage of the sunny river views. An upstairs veranda looked straight down towards his childhood home. Fewer windows on the Quorn Street side protected the house from cold westerly winds,

Clive Lord, date unknown
Libraries Tasmania NS10131-1-1841

he noted. A photograph taken from Quorn Street shows a path from the street, lined with flowering asters, leading to an arched porch. An unnamed woman in a white dress stands awkwardly gesturing to the flowers. That, I think, must have been Doris Lord.

It was a house befitting the leading citizen that Clive Lord was about to become. He was a genial, companionable man by all accounts, a communicator, a networker, an organiser, a careful scientist and a courteous colleague. Aside from his position at the Tasmanian

Museum, the number of organisations he founded, led or was associated with is extraordinary: the Tasmanian Field Naturalists Club (at age fifteen he was a founding member); the Royal Society of Tasmania; the Royal Australasian Ornithologists Union; the Australian Association for the Advancement of Science; the Royal Tasmanian Botanical Gardens; the Mount Field National Park Board; the Australian National Research Council; the Tasmanian Sea Fisheries Board; the Salmon and Freshwater Fisheries Commission; the Tasmanian Institute of Architects; the Hobart Development League; and the Hobart Rotary Club. This is probably not a complete list.

To escape the committee room (and, as we shall see in a moment, a complicated domestic life), Lord sought solitude whenever he could. He climbed Tasmania's mountains and sailed its coastlines. He wrote about Tasmanian birds, fish, marsupials, rodents and snakes, and advocated for the protection of the thylacine. He wrote about Captain William Bligh, Robert Knopwood and Abel Tasman, Tasmanian Aboriginal people, and the histories of Bruny and Maria islands. He journeyed to Mount Field, Lake St Clair and other wilderness places including the remote southwest of the island.

As secretary of the Tasmanian Field Naturalists Club, Lord wrote several reports from its annual Easter camps in the 1920s, including two trips to Port Arthur. This great-great-grandson of a convict wrote in measured tones about Tasmania's convict heritage. Tasmanians at that time tended to either ignore their convict forebears or, at the other extreme, costume them as characters in sensationalised books, films, stage plays and tourist sites. Clive Lord did neither. There was no hiding his own convict origins because his family was too well known, but he deprecated any interest in Port Arthur based on morbid or superficial curiosity. Its history, he believed, was still poorly understood.

In 1926 he published a little booklet, *Some Tasmanian Days*, in which he described some of his travels and indulged a romantic and fanciful side of his nature that sat interestingly alongside the scientific. Dotted through the narrative are snatches of poetry, including this revealing verse from Byron's "Childe Harold's Pilgrimage":

> I live not in myself, but I become
> Portion of that around me; and to me
> High mountains are a feeling, but the hum
> Of human cities torture ...

Lord was made a fellow of the Linnean Society of London in 1922, and in 1930 the Royal Society of Tasmania presented him with its medal for distinguished service to the society and the state. His major scientific achievement was his co-authorship (with H.H. Scott) of the book *A Synopsis of the Vertebrate Animals of Tasmania*, published in 1924. Based on journeys in his yacht *Telopea*, he developed an interest in the European exploration of the Tasmanian coast, and in 1933 had begun a series of radio broadcasts on this subject when he died suddenly of a stroke, aged only forty-three. An accumulation of professional and personal stresses may have been a contributing factor.

I'm saddened to think of Lord's life ending so early. I'm drawn to his energy and commitment, his curiosity and his desire to share knowledge. We spent our formative years in the same place, and not just at my school. As a student at the University of Tasmania I was again passing my days on Lord land because the university is sited on what was originally part of the Lord family holdings. Clive and I crossed paths again at the Tasmanian Museum and Art Gallery, when I began my museum career there as a volunteer in 1989.

I am profoundly interested in this man, but the deeper I look the less I know because he will not return my gaze. My portrait of him in this essay is partial and incomplete, and you will notice me at work: leaning in, standing back, applying empathy here, scepticism there, testing the limits of the sources and probing my own subjectivity. I am working with some dark materials; I want you to know that.

* * *

The first thing that drew my interest was Lord's directorship of the Tasmanian Museum and Art Gallery. There he managed ethnographic

Clive Lord, c. 1920s
Libraries Tasmania NS6192-1-102

collections that had been built around the earlier theft, illegal trade and display of Aboriginal remains. More Aboriginal remains were added to the collection in Lord's time. In 1919 he led an excavation in sand dunes at Eaglehawk Neck, on the Tasman Peninsula, which revealed the remains of about twenty Aboriginal Tasmanians, children through to elderly people. In a scientific paper about the discovery, Lord made special note of two of the skulls, one of which was unusually large and the other unusually thick. Altogether, the find was extremely valuable "from an ethnological standpoint".

In various publications Lord repeated the then-orthodox view that Tasmanian Aboriginal people were nomadic wanderers who represented the most "primitive" human society, a "true old Stone Age type".

This he explained by saying that they used chipped stone implements because they had not "got to" the stage of sharpening them into points. Elsewhere he noted that some stone tools showed "exceptional finish", demonstrations of the "high culture" of the Tasmanians compared to other "stone cultures". He believed that they did not eat scale fish, only shellfish, but he differed from the standard opinion that Aboriginal Tasmanians could not make fire (and were obliged to carry burning embers about with them) by pointing to evidence that they could produce fire using a stick in a groove.

Lord had absorbed most of his knowledge of Tasmanian Aboriginal people from the writings of explorers and early colonists, and from his study of his museum's artefacts. He had no formal training in archaeology and indeed there was no university-based discipline of archaeology in Australia then. However, he was deeply interested in the subject and regretted that so little evidence of the "habits" of the "natives" had been gathered prior to the "extinction" of the "race".

Eager to educate museum visitors, Lord supervised the development of a life-sized group exhibit of Aboriginal Tasmanians – a frozen-in-time diorama of a father, mother and child gathered around a campfire – unveiled to great acclaim in May 1931. The exhibit was considered at the forefront of museum display and the Hobart *Mercury* took great interest. The paper had noted in January 1931 that such exhibits were looked upon by scientists as "the proper way to show objects", instead of being isolated in glass cases "with small relation to ideas".

Lord drew on his research and his own design skills to guide the composition and construction of the exhibit. He also organised for the sculptor E.J. Dicks to have the skeleton of Truganini, the so-called "last Tasmanian", who had died in 1876, set up in his studio at the museum for reference. At the launch of the exhibit in May, one of the museum's trustees, Dr William E. Crowther (himself an avid collector of Aboriginal remains), declared that the hope for the exhibit was that it would strike the imagination of children and allow them "to realise clearly the nature and habits of the aboriginals of Tasmania".

I want to be even-handed here, to say that Lord was trying to do the right thing, that he was a thoughtful and open-minded man and that the group exhibit was a genuine attempt to preserve and educate. Yet he was also complicit in practices that objectified the lives and culture of his fellow humans. The exhibit amplified those practices and made it safe for others to do the same. He explicitly dismissed the continued existence of Aboriginal Tasmanians living on the Bass Strait islands – the "quadroon descendants", as he called them. The exhibit was still on display when I was growing up; I remember it well. Its ultimate effect was to keep Tasmanian Aboriginal people in a distant state of permanent primitiveness, where it was not *needful* for anyone to consider their humanity or the survival of their culture.

Truganini's skeleton remained on display at the museum until at least 1948 and possibly longer. Finally in 1976 it was removed, cremated and scattered in D'Entrecasteaux Channel, which is what she had always wanted. The group exhibit was not removed from display until 2007. For the trauma inflicted by these and many other injustices, the board of the museum offered Tasmania's Aboriginal people a lengthy, formal and public apology in 2021. Clive Lord's life's work was part of what was being apologised for, but I cannot complacently distance myself from that legacy. It is right to reject the racist assumptions prevalent in Lord's time, and it is right that museums return Aboriginal remains to Country where possible. But equally it is right to acknowledge that museum curators today work within the same colonial-era practices of collecting, classifying, naming, controlling and dominating. Lord's acquisitiveness and his thirst for knowledge: I understand them, I share them.

* * *

But when I think of Clive Lord, I don't think of him in his office at the museum in downtown Hobart, but at home in Quorn Street. This house, with its back to the westerly winds and its face to the sun, provided no haven from worry for him because although a successful and well-liked man in public, his home life was painfully difficult.

Clive and Doris had one child, daughter Lois, born in 1919 with severe physical and intellectual disabilities. I discovered this accidentally when I noticed that the Tasmanian Archives holds a file on Lois kept by the State Psychological Clinic. In February 1928, aged nine, Lois was examined by the clinic and assessed as having a mental age of a three-year-old and an IQ of thirty-five. Subsequent tests put her IQ at twenty-six. She was probably assessed as part of routine psychological testing of Tasmanian school children enabled by the state's *Mental Deficiency Act* of 1920.

That legislation was regarded as humanitarian at the time, for it was the first in Australia to distinguish "mental deficiency" from "insanity". Although not backed up by enough funding to establish the institutions of care it envisaged, it took as a premise that, with adequate and specialised support, "mental defectives" could live fulfilling lives. The identification, care and management of mental defectives was much in the public conversation at this time, although not always out of a concern for them as individuals. In the language of eugenics, mental defectives (which could also include criminals, alcoholics and homosexuals) were not considered "useful" to society; they were "socially inefficient". There was still a belief among some eugenicists that there was a direct correlation between the cubic capacity of the brain, measured in skull size, and intelligence. Some advocated the segregation and sterilisation of mental defectives.

I have not found any publicly stated opinion by Clive Lord on eugenics, but there is ample evidence that he moved in the professional circles in which it was discussed, and that he was familiar with the study of the cranium. He does not seem to have come to any conclusions on cranium size and intelligence – perhaps because the whole subject was intensely personal for him. It was personal for me too, although I find it hard to explain why. With quite low expectations I waited for Lois Lord's file to be digitised; with archives, you never know what you are going to get. So I was truly, profoundly shocked when I opened the file and found myself reading this brutal detail:

> Poor physical development – long thin face – narrow highly arched palate – speech very thick and imperfect – restless, talks incessantly and cannot concentrate – flatfooted – could not grasp the nature of the simplest performance processes – fundamental inner auditory and visual processes sub-evolved – cannot handle effectively language mechanisms – makes grimaces – facial tics – infantile babblings ...

And there was a lot more of that, even a cryptic suggestion – apparently made by Doris Lord – that some "mental weakness" was indicated on Lois's "paternal side".

Reading it felt like a terrible intrusion, even though under Tasmania's archives legislation I had every right to see it. I remember snapping shut the laptop and walking restlessly around the house for a long time, unable to describe my emotions but essentially, I suppose, asking myself what would *I* do if I had to cope with a child like that? How would *I* want my child to be treated? It was as if the wall between the present and the past had collapsed, leaving me utterly baffled and confused. But is there really such a wall, I wondered? "The past is never dead. It's not even past." How many times had I read William Faulkner's famous aphorism? Many times, although small use it was now. Still, curiosity had got me this far, so I carried on researching and wondering.

Lois's parents cannot have failed to have noticed her developmental delays, but perhaps it was the intervention of the state that forced a discussion about her future – and a crisis in their marriage. Anxiety, exhaustion, guilt, fear, anger, shame, blame: all these emotions may have taken up residence in the house on Quorn Street. In October 1928 Clive petitioned for divorce on the grounds of Doris's "desertion". Divorce was much rarer then and often reported in the newspaper, which is how I learned about it. He told the Supreme Court that he had been "refused marital relations" by Doris ever since his return from a visit to Mount Field National Park in late 1919. (Lois had been born in January 1919.) Doris's lawyer successfully applied for a permanent order for alimony.

It's possible that the "refusal of marital relations" was a manoeuvre on Doris's part to prevent further children, or it could even have been a mutual arrangement between the couple. If so, Clive obviously grew tired of it and was willing to endure public humiliation to escape. In less than a year he remarried and brought his new bride, Florence Jessie Knight, a former school teacher, to live in the sunny house in Quorn Street. Doris assumed sole care for Lois and set up a household for them both nearby in Proctors Road.

Now that the wall was down, I found myself talking directly to my subject as if he were in the same room. "You shit, Clive Lord, you absolute *shit*. You chuck Doris out on her own with the 24/7 care of a severely disabled child while you carry on as normal with a new wife to give you everything you need." Is that fair? Is that how it was? Could Doris's own anxiety and stress have made life under the one roof unbearable, meaning that Lois was actually better off somewhere else? Clive did do the right thing financially, it would seem, if the evidence of his having sold property he owned in Quorn Street and around the corner in Nelson Road in 1928 is anything to go by. In 1931 he also sold his beloved yacht, *Telopea*.

In 1931 Doris was notified by the Public Health Department that her daughter had been assessed as a "mentally defective child (imbecile class)" and was not "educable", even to the standards of the special classes run by the Education Department. Actually, Lois had been attending a special class at the Elizabeth Street Practising School in North Hobart, but once she was too old for that there was nowhere else she could go. Doris was coolly informed that "unfortunately" there was no school "as yet" in Tasmania for "the more serious retarded cases" such as Lois's.

* * *

So then I wanted to know more about Florence Lord, the second wife. The presence of a (possibly vindictive) first wife and disabled daughter only a few streets away cannot have made her married life easy.

But then, after less than two years, a totally new calamity struck the Lord household.

In 1930 Clive and Florence (always known by her second name, Jessie) billeted in their house a clergyman visiting Hobart for a Church of England synod. The Reverend Alfred Edwin James, recently transferred from New South Wales and now rector of the church in Ellendale in Tasmania's lower midlands, arrived at Quorn Street on 28 April. It was later alleged in court that on the following evening the Lords' maid, an unnamed seventeen-year-old girl, awoke to find him sitting on her bed with his hand under her head. He made "a suggestion" to her which she rejected, and the pair struggled.

Then, according to the girl's testimony, he told her that all would be "quite alright" but that if she called out it would be "harder for her". He then raped her.

The next night he did the same, although this time he brought something in a bottle or a tin and rubbed it on her chest, which made her feel "dizzy" and she fell asleep. The next day the girl told Jessie Lord that she did not like Reverend James. The girl did, however, manage to find a key to her door. The day after that, a Friday, James left.

On Saturday the girl told Jessie the whole story. In May the girl testified before a magistrate that Mrs Lord had said: "You could knock me down with a feather, he being a minister, and interfering with a little girl." Jessie said she had noticed that, from the day after the first incident, the girl was unwell, and one evening Jessie herself had had to prepare the evening meal. On the Saturday Clive moved the girl's bed into another room despite Alfred James having left by then.

Two doctors testified that they had examined the girl and found signs that she had recently been "interfered with", although they differed slightly as to when it could have occurred. Appearing for Alfred James, Albert Ogilvie KC (also a Labor parliamentarian) submitted that the doctors' evidence was not "corroborated" and that a judge could not convict on the girl's own story. The magistrate replied that that was for a jury to decide, and he sent the case to the Supreme Court. The magistrate's hearing received relatively restrained coverage in the Hobart *Mercury*, but the Sydney gossip tabloid *Truth* got hold of it and splashed it across half a page under the headline "Hullo, Darling" (James's alleged greeting to the girl when he entered her room the second night). The paper also reported Jessie's full name and address.

For the criminal trial in July, *Truth* had lost interest but the Tasmanian papers covered it. Acting Solicitor-General Arnold Banks Smith prosecuted, while Albert Ogilvie appeared again for the defence. This time Jessie Lord testified that the Reverend James had asked her if the room at the top of the stairs was the maid's room, which she thought was a "strange question". James denied having asked this and stated that the girl's story was a "dastardly untruth". The prosecution combed through his life history to characterise James as wayward and a drunkard. The same doctors gave the same medical evidence. But the judge summed up by saying that he could not see any "real corroboration" of the evidence, and he suggested to the jury that the "curious errors" made by the girl on "unforgettable matters" made it dangerous for them to accept her evidence unhesitatingly. Members of the jury agreed, and after retiring for just eighteen minutes they returned a verdict of not guilty.

It was the merest chance that the incident occurred in the Lords' house – Jessie stated in court that James was an "absolute stranger" to the household – but still the embarrassment must have been awful. Already Clive had had to allow the family name to be dragged through the divorce court, and now his second wife was being named in the salacious pages of *Truth*. And yet the Lords did not back away from the case. Who else but Clive would have paid the girl's legal and medical expenses? It would probably have been easier to hush the whole thing up and hustle the girl back to her family, but he did not.

One of the doctors who examined her was Dr Wendell Inglis Clark (who, a year later, would be one of the specialists who undertook the psychological testing on Lois Lord). Wendell was the son of a prominent professional family in Hobart and a friend of William Crowther.

The other doctor was Dr Christine Walch, a recognised advocate for women's health and daughter of a successful Hobart bookseller. I feel the mind of Clive Lord at work here, trying to do the right thing, assembling a pair of experts from among his connections in Hobart's intellectual and forward-thinking circles. If so, his efforts failed to tip the massive power imbalance between a clergyman of the Church of England and a seventeen-year-old servant girl.

The Reverend Alfred James returned to New South Wales and served in many parishes until his death at Boggabri in 1947 of heart disease. He had made much of having served in the First World War, but in 1940 the Armidale RSL quietly made enquiries based on local suspicions that James had not actually gone to war after all. Defence authorities in Melbourne confirmed that he had served with the YMCA as an "Hon. Captain" attached to the Second Light Horse Regiment, but they had no other particulars of his service. His service file, now held by the National Archives of Australia, does not contain any of the standard military records, such as an attestation paper or a service and casualty form, which is most unusual. There was something odd about this man. At his memorial service in Armidale in 1947, a fellow cleric acknowledged that James's life had been hard, and he had not been perfect, but that "he had carried his cross courageously". Exactly what that cross had been was left unstated.

In all three of these episodes in the life of Clive Lord, I find myself suggesting that he was trying to do the "right thing", possibly without knowing what the right thing was. And here is me, also trying to do the right thing by explaining how Lord tried to do the right thing, but I also don't know what that is. Obviously, he doesn't care what I think. We have a shared place, Clive and I, but when I journey there to meet him, he declines to meet with me.

* * *

The Royal Society of Tasmania still awards a medal in Clive Lord's memory, but no-one is awarding medals in memory of the women in his life. So let me offer the few details I have about what happened to them, and we'll leave it there.

After her divorce in 1928 Doris Lord stayed on in Hobart for several years, but eventually returned to Sydney with Lois and found a flat in Gore Hill. There, closer to her own family, she might have had more options for Lois's care. Lois died in 1950, aged thirty-one. Doris remained in Gore Hill and died in 1960, aged seventy-two. Her will suggests that she had been financially comfortable, living off investments. Whether or not Lois had lived with her or in an institution is unclear, but a £250 legacy to the New South Wales Society for Crippled Children suggests that Lois had been helped by them.

Jessie Lord did not remarry after Clive's death in 1933, living quietly in Quorn Street for many years. Complete obscurity must have been what she sought because she never appeared in the social pages, not even for so much as running a stall at a church fete. After 1954 I lose track of her until her death in a Hobart nursing home in 1986, aged ninety-five, after fifty-three years of widowhood.

Vanished altogether is the unnamed seventeen-year-old girl at the centre of the rape case who, while still a child, stood up in court in front of all those powerful members of Hobart's elite. Her case lost, she entered that vast and ever-expanding sisterhood of women whose testimonies are not believed.

The Telegram

Gunner E.R. Garriock Fourth Field Artillery ... killed in action 15/9/17. Please inform father Mr T. Garriock ... Duke Place Balmain reply paid ...

Duke Place is a tiny street in East Balmain, Sydney. Poor people don't live there any more, but once this district was home to people working in the factories and dockyards around Mort Bay. Thomas Garriock was a labourer, and his son Eric was a plumber who had enlisted in the Australian Imperial Force in 1915.

The telegram had been sent on 9 October 1917 to the Reverend George Cranston, the minister at the Presbyterian church in Campbell Street, Balmain. It was his job to break the news of Eric's death to the Garriock family. He probably delayed his call until the late afternoon, when Thomas would be home from work and his wife Ann, Eric's mother, would not be alone. So: a house, a doorstep, a nervous clergyman with a duty to perform.

As he stood there, he might have smelled dinner cooking and heard the Garriock daughters chatting as they helped their mother. The oldest girl, Ora, had married in 1917, but Agnes, Annie and Robina were still at home. Their father was perhaps sitting in the corner with the evening paper. People often dreaded the sight of a clergyman in their street, and Reverend Cranston might already have been seen walking up Duke Place. Whose turn was it this time?

While life had thus carried on as usual at Duke Place, Eric had been dead for three weeks. He had given "Presby" as his religion when he enlisted, so it was up to his local Presbyterian minister to offer any comfort the family would accept. Breaking the news to nonbelievers, a clergyman could find himself back on the street in no time. But George Cranston and Thomas Garriock were fellow Scots, and perhaps this was enough to give Cranston entry to the household even if the Garriocks were not regular churchgoers.

It might also have helped that Cranston was a former army chaplain and had served sixteen months overseas in Egypt and France. Faced with the Garriocks' pleading eyes, he didn't need to rely on empty platitudes: he would have ministered to many dying men, buried them, and written letters home to their families.

What most people wanted was the truth, however brutal. How did my son die? Where is he buried? Who was with him at the end? Cranston had no more information for the Garriocks that day than was in the telegram, but he would at least have been able to respond with something authentic from his own experience. Then, after leaving the telegram with the family, he would have walked back to the manse and to his wife, Marion. "Don't hold dinner," he probably would have said on his way out. "I don't know how long I'll be."

* * *

What happened next? At this distance it is near impossible to know how grief played out in the lives of the Garriocks, and how long was the shadow it cast. This was not a well-off family with the leisure to preserve their feelings in letters and diaries. So, let's come at it from another angle.

What happened to the telegram? Such a flimsy piece of paper for the weight of news it carried. Was it abandoned on the kitchen table? Did it flutter to the floor? Or did the family pore over it, searching for answers? Tens of thousands of similar messages were delivered all over the country between 1915 and 1918. What did people *do* with them? Is it something you would throw out, like a gas bill? How could you, with the words "killed in action" next to your son's name?

In 1987, seventy years after this telegram was received, it was donated to the Australian War Memorial. If you order it up to the reading room today, you are presented with a carefully preserved piece of paper in an acid-free cardboard folder. In researching this essay I found about ten official First World War telegrams like this at the Memorial, contained within small collections donated by families. Typically, these collections might include some letters and cards home from the soldier, condolence letters after his death, commemorative memorabilia, information about his burial, a notebook or pocket diary, photographs and newspaper clippings. What families donate varies according to time and circumstances, and as a researcher in the reading room you learn never to build too many hopes.

Knowing this, I was still taken aback when I opened the Garriock folder to find just this solitary piece of paper. I was tempted to shake the folder in case something else dropped out. Is this record any less weighted with meaning than those more elaborate collections? I took a second look. The telegram bears the marks of having once been folded and carried around for a long time, resulting in tears along the creases and one of the folded surfaces becoming more rubbed than the others. Perhaps someone carried it in a wallet? It was probably Thomas (the father), not Ann (the mother), because women carried purses in those days, not wallets. Was that a strange thing to do? Who can say?

In pencil on the back of the telegram, these words have been written in a small neat hand:

Dock Rs 1st 2 of storey house past Bay St

Directions to some waterfront location? Not the Garriocks' own house, for there is no Bay Street in the area. Perhaps Thomas made the jotting himself when he needed to note something down and the telegram was all he had.

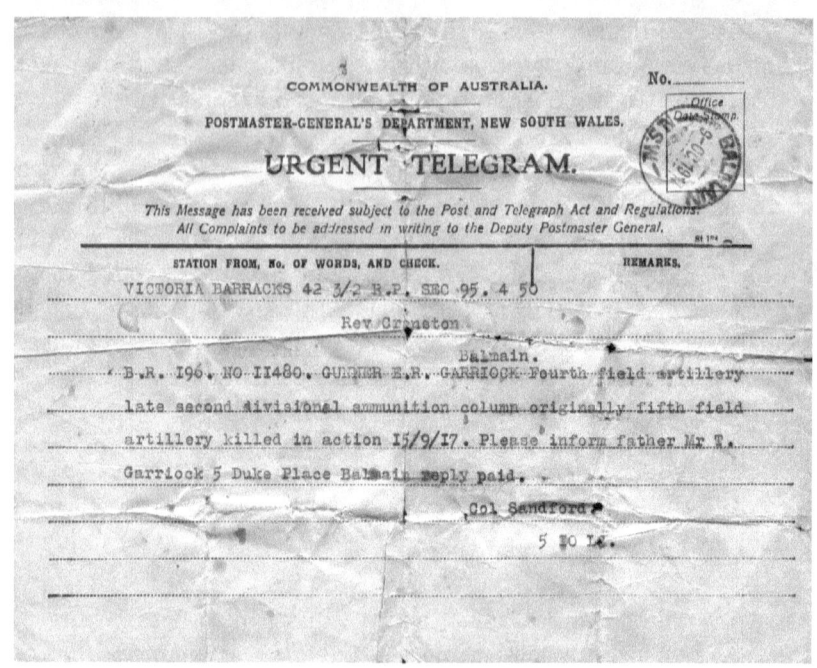

Telegram announcing the death of Eric Garriock, 1917
Australian War Memorial AWM2020.7.96

* * *

I wanted more context. I pulled up Eric's war service record, which is held by the National Archives of Australia and viewable online. He died in one of the battles of 1917 known collectively as the Third Battle of Ypres. I was interested in any evidence of how his family dealt with news of his death and noticed that, unusually, no personal items were returned to them. A deceased soldier's kit was always examined and anything not issued by the AIF was sent to his family, who were always anxious to receive anything, however trivial, as mementos. Soldiers couldn't carry or store much stuff, but most had something: a wallet, a Bible, a few photographs, perhaps a pocket diary. But Eric's service record notes that when he died he had no personal effects at all.

However, as next of kin Thomas Garriock was issued with Eric's service medals and the commemorative bronze plaque and scroll sent to all families of the British Empire war dead. Also standard was an official photograph of the soldier's grave, if there was one (many soldiers' remains were never found). These photographs showed the temporary grave, usually marked by a simple wooden cross, and were mounted in cardboard folders with the precise location of the grave given. Relatives could draw comfort from this information even though few could ever expect to visit the grave.

A photograph of Eric's grave was sent to Thomas by defence authorities in May 1920 and he replied to say how pleased he was, but he apologised that he could not afford to "improve" the grave. By that he probably meant that he would not be able to pay for an inscription once his son's remains were permanently marked under a headstone. All headstones included the soldier's name, military unit and date of death, but any personal inscriptions had to be paid for by the family. The cost was thruppence ha'penny per letter for a maximum of sixty-six letters including spaces. Historian Colin Bale has estimated that the cost of a full inscription would be about a quarter of a basic adult weekly wage. At least a third of Australian identified graves have no personal inscription.

Thomas was so troubled about his inability to pay for an inscription that he wrote in 1922, unprompted, to apologise again. He had been invalided after an accident in 1917, he explained, and when his wife died in 1921 the twelve-shilling weekly pension paid to her as a dependent of Eric's was stopped. Thomas was living near Gloucester in northern New South Wales by then and relied on "the daughters" for everything he received. "I hope the country won't forget the Boys who gave their lives for their King and Country," he wrote. Maybe that was the inscription he'd have chosen: "For King and Country." Eric's final resting place is in the Birr Cross Roads Cemetery, three kilometres east of Ypres, Belgium. Thomas Garriock died in 1946.

* * *

With archives, abundance is always regarded as a virtue. Breadth, depth, richness, variety: that's what we want, and get, in the great deposits of personal records. The papers of John Monash, probably Australia's most famous soldier, occupy sixty metres of shelving at the National Library of Australia and another six metres at the Australian War Memorial. Many biographies have been written from them. Biographers' careers can be built on access to rich deposits like these. Subject, biographer and the holding institution can all bask in a mutual glow of prestige and influence.

But fat biographies lull us into false expectations. What is actually held in archives and museums represents the merest fraction of the material evidence created in a society at any given time. Novelist Hilary Mantel expresses it best. History, she says, is "what's left in the sieve when the centuries have run through it – a few stones, scraps of writing, scraps of cloth".

How then do we grapple with scarcity, not abundance? We must begin with an awareness that many processes and circumstances are at play in the creation of records and their preservation as archives. Our man Eric Garriock probably did write at least a few letters or cards home to his family and it's obvious from his enlistment papers that he could write – but these have not come to light, nor has the photograph of his grave that we know existed. If he had a studio photograph taken in uniform before he left Australia, as many excited young enlistees did, it has not been donated to a public collection and neither have his service medals and the memorial plaque and scroll.

And the telegram? It has little obvious evidential value. By the time it was donated in 1987, the Memorial had long since collected the details of all the Australian First World War dead for its Roll of Honour in Canberra, so the telegram added nothing to the existing public record.

What about the file documenting the Garriock acquisition by the Memorial? That too is slender. It shows that the donor was a Mrs W. Bentley of Punchbowl, New South Wales. The only other item in the deposit is a piece of souvenir embroidery from Egypt with "From Eric to Agnes" inscribed in stitches. Such souvenirs were cheap to personalise, and Eric obviously sent one home to his sister while he trained at a camp near Cairo in early 1916.

The file contains nothing to indicate this Mrs Bentley's connection with the Garriock family. Who was she? Electoral records show that Agnes Garriock, Eric's sister, remained unmarried and lived in Punchbowl for many years, so Mrs Bentley may have been a younger friend who, on Agnes's death in 1970, received some of her possessions. But while she cared enough to offer the telegram and the embroidery to the Australian War Memorial, she may have known very little about them. No story – no anecdotes about Agnes or her long-dead brother – came with the donation, leaving us to suppose that too many years had passed and there was nothing left to say. The emotion of that frightful moment in 1917 on the doorstep at the little house in Duke Place had all been spent.

The embroidery does yield a story of its own, though. It has been mounted on a stiff brown backing, and over many years light has faded the dyes in the fabric, turning red into pink and blue to pale grey. You can see the original colours around the edges where the mount has crumbled and flaked away. This deterioration would have been arrested once the object was placed in museum storage. So? Agnes Garriock must have had it on the wall in her house for so many years it almost fell apart in front of her eyes.

They that are left grow old, and so does the material evidence of their loves and sorrows.

* * *

For Reverend Cranston, the Garriock telegram would have been one of dozens he had to deliver after his return from his own overseas service in March 1917. It was part of any parish priest's or clergyman's duties. Policy on this appears to have been formulated around the time the nation began to brace itself for the first casualties from

Embroidered souvenir sent home by Eric Garriock, 1916
Australian War Memorial REL/15746

the Dardanelles (Gallipoli). On 29 April 1915, defence minister George Pearce told the Senate that relatives of soldiers reported missing or killed would receive the news via a telegram delivered by a clergyman of the soldier's denomination. (In the 1911 census, less than 1 per cent of the Australian population had declared themselves non-Christian.) The names of the dead would then appear in the official casualty lists published in newspapers. Pearce's announcement was reported in the press the next day.

In Britain and Germany, by contrast, messenger boys delivered the telegram, a terrible burden to place on the shoulders of boys aged not even eighteen. Many of them probably handed over the piece of paper and rode off on their bicycles as fast as they could. The system in Australia was more humane, but there were still flaws. Sometimes the clergyman couldn't break the news because the family was not living at the given address. In 1916 this was reportedly happening in about one in ten cases, which is why Base Records, the office set up in Melbourne by the defence department to handle soldiers' records and coordinate casualty notifications, constantly pleaded with people to keep their addresses up to date. The ultimate horror was that families would read about a death in the newspaper, which did sometimes happen. Clergymen were required to notify authorities when they had delivered the message to each family so that the names could go forward for publication, but there were a few who did this immediately, only to discover that the telegram was undeliverable.

For years I wondered how this whole system had worked. Clergymen broke the news, yes, but how did they know who had died, and where to call? Finally in 2019 I found the procedure described in an obscure defence department report published in 1917. A telegram was sent by Base Records in Melbourne to the military district in which the soldier had enlisted (the 2nd, in Eric's case, which was New South Wales), and the commandant there authorised a telegram to the relevant clergyman. Back at Base Records, a small note was made on the soldier's file that the necessary action had been taken. So, on Eric's file we read: "Oct 8 1917 MC2 advised killed in action 15/9/17." But you must be very sharp-eyed to notice it.

In making clergymen into foot soldiers for the state, the government relied on the cooperation of churches, and for the most part got it. But people's dread of noticing a clergyman in their street impeded clergymen's normal parish visiting and before long, many of them began to regard the whole business as a terrible ordeal. Michael McKernan, one of the few Australian historians to have studied this aspect of home front history, corresponded with the son of a wartime clergyman who told him that his father had found the work "extremely distressing" and "never forgot how it hurt".

* * *

The urge to make a story out of these slivers and fragments is irresistible. I keep probing the Garriock story from different angles, this way and that, searching, as novelists and biographers do, for hints to fill gaps and absences. I want to give Eric Garriock's life some meaning apart from the fact of his early death. The Australian War Memorial was founded in the 1920s and 1930s as a national repudiation of meaninglessness: what parent can accept that their child's death was pointless? That is why it built its collections with such relentless determination in those early years, and why the quiet simplicity of the building in Canberra was so important. There had to be solace *somewhere*, surely?

But no mountain of paper or pile of stones will bring back the dead. The Garriock telegram confronts us with the terrible mystery of death. He breathed, and then he didn't. He is not coming home.

Infantrymen near the battlefront during the Third Battle of Ypres, 1917
Photographer: Frank Hurley
Australian War Memorial E00846

The Names Inlaid

> *No matter how small*
> *Every town has one;*
> *Maybe just the obelisk,*
> *A few names inlaid;*
> *More often full-scale granite,*
> *Marble digger (arms reversed),*
> *Long descending lists of dead:*
> *Sometimes not even a town,*
> *A thickening of houses*
> *Or a few unlikely trees*
> *Glimpsed on a back road*
> *Will have one.*
>
> Geoff Page, "Smalltown Memorials"

When Geoff Page published "Smalltown Memorials" in 1975, its elegiac tone resonated with readers worried that the rituals of Anzac were fading from Australian life. Perhaps, it was thought, Anzac commemorations wouldn't outlast the passing of the last veteran of the First World War?

The poem reminds me of country drives. You stop for a break, and on the way back to the car you glance across at the town's war memorial and frown, wondering if you should pause. If someone had the decency to put a memorial there – no, if someone had the decency to volunteer for war in the first place – the least you can do is spend five minutes having a look.

You wander over to read the names inlaid, and marvel at the men, obviously from the same family, who all joined up, quite possibly breaking their parents' hearts. You circle the memorial respectfully, so as not to neglect names from later conflicts or the names of the occasional Boer War man or army nurse. But the wind whips up and you go back to the car. Doors shut, you turn up the music and get on your way.

A curious traveller might pull out their phone. There are websites dedicated to Australian war memorials and monuments, and a few taps will also bring you the service record of every Australian enlistee in both world wars, held by the National Archives of Australia.

Twenty-three years after Page's poem came the pivotal academic work on war memorials, historian Ken Inglis's masterly *Sacred Places: War memorials in the Australian landscape* (written with Jan Brazier). Despite those earlier fears, interest in Anzac, and in the history of the First World War especially, has not withered. Quite the contrary: our last man might have long passed away, but his memory is kept alive by many, many commemorative shillings.

"Every town has one ..." Yes, so it feels, as if small-town and suburban memorials have always dotted the Australian landscape. And yet there must have been a time during the First World War when *no* town had one, when *no* names were inlaid. What did families do when they began, painfully, to accept that the empty place at the dinner table would never be filled? How would the memory of their son or husband be kept alive?

* * *

Historians have written extensively about mourning and commemorative practices in Australia during and after the First World War, and about whether and how they brought consolation to the bereaved. These are not new questions, and indeed they were not in the front of my mind when by chance I came across a photograph of a woman named Fanny Cooper in the Australian War Memorial's collection. This studio photo with her son Louis was taken in Launceston shortly after he enlisted in October 1916.

It was the image of Fanny that gave me pause. I wondered instantly who this beautiful, sad-eyed woman could possibly be. She seemed old enough to be Louis's grandmother rather than his mother. Patient resignation is written on her face, as if she has known tragedy and is steeling herself for more. And it came. Louis served on the Western Front with the 12th Battalion, Australian Imperial Force, but in July 1918 he died of bronchopneumonia in a military hospital in England. Such is the ready availability of records these days that it took very little effort to establish these facts. The lad in the photograph did not come home. What then of his mother?

Fanny Cooper with her son Louis, 1916
Photographer: S. Spurling
Australian War Memorial P07687.001

The Coopers lived in Longford, a small town about a twenty-minute drive south of Launceston. The family made no special mark on history and apparently left no personal letters or diaries in public archives or libraries. But the National Archives holds Louis's pay file and service records, and in these I found a few letters from Fanny to military authorities seeking information about this and that. Not much, and little to tell me about her life or character.

Now fully immersed in this story, I kept digging and turned, inevitably, to local newspapers. The Launceston papers (the *Examiner* and the

47

Daily Telegraph) routinely covered events in this and other northern districts. Digitised newspapers now make this work astoundingly quick, and this is how I recovered the Cooper family's war story.

Fanny was the daughter of Isaiah Briggs, a saddler by trade and stalwart of Longford's Methodist church, and his wife, Maria. One of Fanny's sisters married the brother of Walter Lee, a Longford man from a Methodist family that ran a business making agricultural implements. Lee rose to prominence as a Tasmanian parliamentarian and, as Sir Walter Lee, was three-time premier of the state. Fanny married William Cooper, a painter and decorator, in 1880. Large families were still common then; Fanny was one of ten children, and she and William had six sons and five daughters. All eleven survived infancy, but their daughter Elsie died of typhoid in 1904, aged seventeen, and in 1910 two of their grandsons died in a horrific fire, aged just six and four.

Louis was the only one of Fanny's sons to enlist, but by the time he did, seven of her nephews had enlisted and three had died. It is no wonder that, by then, Fanny looked all of her fifty-seven years.

* * *

The Coopers were at their property at Liffey when the dreaded telegram arrived in July 1918, announcing Louis's death. For some years the family had divided their time between Longford and Liffey. The Liffey River drains the cliffs of Tasmania's Great Western Tiers and meets the Meander River near Carrick. It is an area of wild beauty, known today for its protected wilderness areas and especially for the famous Liffey Falls. In the Coopers' time, families ran small farms in the valley, grew vegetables and fruit, and trapped rabbits and marsupials for their fur.

The Cooper property appears to have been a mixture of farm and orchard, and provided extra income and employment for the Cooper sons beyond the family painting-and-decorating business in Longford.

The Coopers sent Louis and perhaps some of their youngest children to the school at Liffey, but although there is a Baptist church there the Coopers worshipped at the Methodist church in nearby Bracknell, where William was a lay preacher.

Among the first things William and Fanny did after hurrying back to Longford was place an "In Memoriam" notice for Louis in the *Daily Telegraph*, headed "Duty nobly done". A few weeks later, at Bracknell on 16 August 1918, a memorial tree-planting was held at the recreation ground. Premier Sir Walter Lee attended the event, along with local councillors and clergy, and addressed the crowd. His wife, Margaret, planted the first tree in honour of Colin Saunders, killed at the landing on Gallipoli, who was the district's first soldier to die. The relatives of twelve other soldiers then planted trees, the last one being for Louis Cooper. He had not been dead a month at that point. His parents must still have been reeling.

This was several years – many years, in some cases – before permanent war memorials began to be established in Australian towns and cities. Ken Inglis has noted that expenditure on lavish monuments was discouraged during the war because all fundraising was directed to the war effort. Afterwards, local communities took so long to raise the money and settle upon the form and the location for their memorials that it was too late, Inglis thought, for them to serve as sites of immediate healing or consolation for many bereaved relatives. Anzac and Remembrance Day observances were still only in a formative state.

In the meantime, families needed something, somewhere to go, something to do, beyond their private grieving. This is what a funeral is for, after all. The Coopers and 60,000 other families had no body to bury or funeral to arrange, and no-one knew when or how permanent memorials would be established. So tree-plantings must have been a response to a hunger for ritual.

In Tasmania in the spring of 1918, with the war still going on, public tree-plantings were occurring all over the state – in fifty towns, according to one estimate. The trees were usually planted along major roads as "soldiers' avenues". They drew on a longer-standing practice: community tree-plantings as civic beautification projects had been a feature of Empire Day celebrations each 24 May, possibly based on an American tradition known as Arbor Day. Australia's nationwide tree-planting movement – both to encourage enlistment and to mark the sacrifice of men from the district who had volunteered and died – began in 1916, promoted by returned soldiers' associations and state recruiting committees. A major memorial avenue of 520 trees was established on Hobart's Queen's Domain in 1918 and 1919. These were planted solely for the dead, but in some towns there were plantings for all known volunteers.

Not a huge amount of money or coordination was required to clear and prepare land to establish soldiers' avenues, and councils or local committees raised the funds to cover the costs of trees, tree guards and name plates or boards. Although they were usually secular affairs, a local clergyman would typically make a speech, and there would be hymns. "O God, Our Help in Ages Past" was the most popular, and the assembled crowds would salute the flag and sing the national anthem.

Tree-plantings didn't have to be gloomy. The town of Cressy, about ten kilometres south of Longford, was described as "en fête" for the planting of its sixty trees, and the ceremony at Exton featured games and races for the children. People were often encouraged to support the latest national war loan, and a word of thanks would be put in for the Red Cross. Families gathered for photographs. Children might help with the grubby work of planting the trees, although surely no-one in these rural towns minded getting a bit of dirt on their knees. Proceedings invariably concluded with an afternoon tea provided by a committee of local women.

About 150 trees were planted along several of Longford's major streets on 24 August 1918, with Premier Lee again in attendance. He paid tribute to the bereaved parents of the district and declared his belief that trees were a much better way of "keeping green" the memory of those who had enlisted than the "rearing of a marble monument", because the trees "would grow and live for many years". The names were too numerous to be noted by the local press, but it seems likely that Louis Cooper was among those memorialised. Anyone who had "a boy at the front" could plant a tree as long as they promised to look after it.

Less than a month later, on the grounds of the Liffey state school on 15 September 1918, the Coopers had yet another tree-planting to attend. Basil Archer – a member of the Longford Municipal Council, Methodist lay preacher and scion of one of northern Tasmania's wealthy landowning families – did the honours this time. Again, the first tree was dedicated to Colin Saunders. (Five Saunders men – four brothers and a cousin – had enlisted and three had died, a fact that was probably the stuff of legend in the district.) A tree was planted for Louis Cooper.

As years passed, though, most soldiers' avenues, even the large one in Hobart, fell into disrepair. Relatives who had tended to "their boy's" tree, who had gathered there to spend a moment remembering, or even to have a picnic, gradually moved away or died. Councils ceased to pay attention. Trees died or were cut down to make way for other developments. Guards and name boards were lost. Memories were not "kept green". Rather than being "inlaid" the names were usually painted, impermanently, on timber.

At some point Longford's council removed the name boards for refurbishment, after which they were forgotten and finally disposed of, apparently with no record kept. Were it not for newspaper reports, the existence of many soldiers' avenues would be almost impossible to trace. In 2015 the little community in Liffey replanted their commemorative trees on the site of the old ones, and marked each with a new metal plate. Likewise, volunteers in Hobart have restored the soldiers' avenue and launched a website explaining the history of this and other Tasmanian avenues. It keeps the memory digital.

* * *

Tree-plantings were one form of community response to the loss of sons and husbands.

Honour boards were another, and were unveiled in churches, schools, workplaces and community halls: hundreds in Tasmania, thousands across the country. Most consisted of lists of names painted onto a timber plaque, or "tablet" as they were sometimes called, perhaps embellished with elaborate carvings. Some were merely painted or printed on paper and framed. As with soldiers' avenues, the same names would be repeated in different places, or sometimes omitted entirely for reasons impossible to recover now. No official coordination was undertaken, and few precedents or traditions existed. People just did what they felt was right.

Louis Cooper is named on a large printed honour board dedicated to hundreds of men of the Longford district, which includes enlistments as well as deaths. It looks like a commercial effort by a publishing company, and evidently someone who was not local has gathered the names because all five of the Saunders men are erroneously called Sanders.

The same mistake was not made on the honour roll for fifteen men from Liffey's state school (now a community hall), which includes the Saunders men as well as Louis Cooper. A more elaborate board dedicated to "the mothers in sympathy and in memory of those sons from Longford who fell during the Great War" was unveiled in Longford in 1920. Twenty-six men are named, including Louis and two cousins, Guy Briggs and Charles Lee. Curiously, Louis was not included on the Bracknell town honour board even though his parents planted a tree for him there.

He is named on the honour board unveiled at the Mountain Vale Methodist Church, however. A settlement principally based on sawmilling grew up in this area south of Liffey, towards Blackwood Creek, in the 1860s. The church served as a school building as well. Although the village was in decline by the early twentieth century, fifteen volunteers, including Louis Cooper, are recorded on the honour board. Six

The former Liffey state school, 2021
Photographer: Edward Condé

had died. The church has been dismantled and the honour roll is now kept at the Liffey Baptist Church.

Back in Longford, in May 1922 a memorial window was unveiled at the Methodist church, commemorating the loss of Louis Cooper and six other men from the parish. After the hymns and addresses, the assembled stood in silent prayer as Basil Archer drew aside the Union Jack to reveal the window. Its central feature is a crusader in armour with sword and crown, surrounded by the words "Faithful unto Death" and "I Have Fought the Good Fight".

* * *

Longford's permanent war memorial was finally unveiled in Victoria Park, in the centre of town, in August 1922. It is a black granite obelisk with fifty-three names inlaid, including Louis Cooper's. By then his name had been honoured with three tree-plantings, three honour boards and a church window, meaning that the Coopers had put his name forward for commemorative projects no fewer than eight times in four years. I have no doubt they and their family attended every single planting and unveiling.

We can read accounts of all these events, but we can only imagine the social interactions: the greetings among neighbours and extended kin, the consoling hand on a shoulder, the stories told in odd moments between formalities. Ageing parents listen eagerly to men who had been to the war and come back, keen for anything that could help them understand how their son had died. Over cups of tea, they might grumble about how slow military authorities were to pass on information, but they might also share some of their son's letters and mementos, perhaps even a pocket diary sent home with his last effects. Clergymen murmur words of consolation. Young men who had not volunteered stand apart, talking among themselves. Children dodge about, gobbling cake while trying to look solemn.

Community events like this gave the bereaved a space within which to renew social connections and compose a story of the war that they could live with. They would see roughly the same people and hear the same speeches from the same local worthies at events held sometimes only weeks apart. The very repetition might have been comforting. Everyone had heard all the rhetoric before, of course, but that wouldn't have mattered. Seeing their boy's name listed in public among the others was what mattered. If that helped to define and externalise their loss, a path towards acceptance might just have been possible.

As Fanny and Louis Cooper posed for their photograph in late 1916, she in her best dress and he in his newly issued uniform, Fanny must have known that her Louis might not come back. Other women in her community, including her own sisters, had already been bereaved by then. How could any parent live with that awful uncertainty? That is the mystery preserved in the photograph; that is what draws our eyes to hers.

Unquiet Stories from Liffey

The cemetery wasn't our main destination. My son Eddie and I had left Hobart that morning and travelled up the Midland Highway through Ross and Campbell Town as far as Powranna (population twenty-five), where we took the back roads through the little towns of Cressy and Bracknell to Liffey. We were looking for the old Liffey school. But we also knew from the map we'd bought in Hobart that there was a cemetery in Liffey, and I absolutely cannot go past an old cemetery without pausing for a look.

Although I grew up in Hobart I had never been to this part of Tasmania before. Liffey is a very beautiful place, not a town but a cluster of small properties following the valley of the Liffey River. The cemetery is clearly marked on the map, but on the ground a cemetery without a church is an easy thing to miss. Suddenly, a glimpse of white showed above the tall yellow grass – white where there shouldn't have been any white. We pulled over.

The cemetery's double iron gates have crosses worked into them, signalling that this is consecrated ground. A lichen-encrusted sign told us that the Mountain Vale Methodist Church occupied the site from 1867 until 1952. Behind us was Mountain Vale Hill, and across some green paddocks to the west, rearing up grimly on the other side of the Liffey River, were the densely forested Cluan Tiers.

We stomped through a patch of long grass and Scotch thistles, where the church must have stood, and past the remnants of a paling fence. The tall white headstone we'd seen from the road turned out to belong to Bertram Henry Saunders, who died in 1906 aged nineteen, and his sister Lily, who died in 1910 aged twenty-eight. Inscribed on their headstone is a pair of clasped hands surrounded by leaves and flowers. We could only see about twenty marked graves, none more recent than the 1930s. All were humbler than the marble headstone dedicated to young Bertram and Lily Saunders, reaching out above the grass to beg passers-by that this place not be forgotten.

* * *

Saunders. I recognised the name. I'd been researching the impact of the First World War in this district and I knew that five men named Saunders had enlisted from around here, and that they feature on local war memorials. Bertram and Lily had to have been from that family. War memorials were why we had come. For the previous essay in this book I wanted photographs of trees which had been planted in 2015 at the old Liffey school. Those trees replaced ones planted in 1918 in honour of the men from Liffey who had volunteered for war. That done, we'd be on our way. We were snatching a few days' holiday over Easter and would be spending that night in Longford.

But you can't stand in an old cemetery, as we were doing, and not wonder about the entire history of the place and the people, and whether, after all, war was the defining event in their lives. I could see by the dates that these must have been some of the first white settler families in this district. Some had sent grandsons and sons to the war; others – whose names I did not recognise from local war memorials – had obviously not.

Anzac has narrowed our focus. It reduces our questions to those that treat the war as an inevitability. But it was not inevitable for Bertram and Lily, who died before 1914. These young people died quite innocent of one of the twentieth century's great tragedies. The war, so soon

The Saunders family grave at Liffey, 2021
Photographer: Edward Condé

to grind itself into Australia's national psyche, never happened for them. Glancing up and around, I began to wonder about the long history of this place and the complex human stories that might be folded into those hills. Overwhelmed with curiosity, I would gladly have got down on my knees, right there and then, and scraped though thistles and bare earth if only that would have revealed these people's lives to me. What else happened here? How did the land and environment shape people's ambitions, work and family life? Investigating this might produce histories that don't sit comfortably with one another.

* * *

The headwaters of the Liffey River gather in Tasmania's Great Western Tiers and take a wild course through rainforest before plunging down four magnificent cascades known collectively as the Liffey Falls. The river is close to the boundaries of three nations of Tasmanian Aboriginal people, and several clans within these nations once made seasonal journeys through the area. Of these, the Pallittorre clan of the North nation was based at Quamby Bluff, a prominent nearby mountain peak not far from Liffey Falls.

On 24 June 1827 a group of Pallittorre people camped between the Liffey Falls (then known as Laycock Falls) and Quamby Bluff. They woke late in the evening to the barking of their dogs. Their fires had revealed their location to five white settlers – two soldiers, a police constable and two stockmen – intent upon reprisal for the murder the previous day of a white stockman, William Knight. The settlers fired on the Pallittorre people as they ran into the bush.

Depositions given the following week in Launceston by two of the settlers stated that only one round was fired on the Aboriginal people (many more on their dogs) and that one person had been wounded. But the Hobart *Colonial Times* reported – almost gleefully – that up to sixty Aboriginal people had been "killed and wounded". Historians who have studied the incident accept that a massacre took place. Killings continued on both sides in the ensuing days, part of what

Victoria Falls near Liffey, c. 1940s
Libraries Tasmania AA193/1/1562

historian Lyndall Ryan has called an "eighteen-day killing spree" in June 1827.

The Pallittorre survivors may have been too frightened to return to the killing sites to observe funerary customs over the dead. Their normal practice was to cremate bodies, but fires would yet again have given away their location. Without these rites, the spirits of the dead would never rest. In later years, stockmen and timber cutters passing through might have heard stories about the killing of the "Blacks", might even have found a few bones here and there. Today, no memorials mark the sites near Liffey where the Pallittorre people died.

* * *

By the 1860s land outside Tasmania's central midland corridor had been opened up for closer settlement. In Liffey, one of the first white arrivals was James Green, and it was he who donated a sliver of land for the building of the Methodist church in 1867, naming it Mountain Vale after his own property. Timber for the church was cut at his steam sawmill. The structure was so austere you might have almost mistaken it for a barn, not a church. A flourishing community grew up around it, and every year, for many years, Green gave his workers a day off so that they and their families could celebrate the founding of the church.

Most of the blocks sold or leased in Liffey were just a few hundred acres each and located in difficult country. Fertile, certainly, but densely timbered, wet, very cold in winter and remote from markets for the settlers' produce. Clearing enough land to establish a viable farm could take a lifetime, but landholders were at least entitled to vote in local and colonial elections, and this gave them some say in the sort of society they wanted to live in. Until then much of the colony's best land had been granted to free immigrants with plenty of capital who had used convict labour to establish vast pastoral estates. But now, new generations of settlers were pushing into "new" country and helping to level out old social inequalities.

The Saunders family, I discovered, were among that cohort. There were two couples: Caroline and John Saunders, and Maria and William Saunders. Caroline and Maria were sisters, and their husbands were probably cousins. Such couplings were not uncommon. Caroline and Maria's parents, Jane and John Jones, had taken up land in Liffey in 1863. John Jones was killed by a falling tree while he was building a house for his young family.

* * *

Caroline and John Saunders married in 1881 and had ten children. Eventually they did well enough to build a six-room farmhouse, quite fine for Liffey then, which they called Silverburn, but like many bush families they probably started out in a simple timber hut. With too many people living in unsanitary conditions, disease was common. Rose, their third-born, died of typhoid in 1884 at just ten months. She was probably buried in the Mountain Vale cemetery under a simple wooden cross, but if so, the grave marker is long gone. Bertram and Lily at least survived to adulthood. I don't know what carried them off, tuberculosis perhaps. By then, the Saunders parents could afford an elaborately carved headstone for them. Unusually for a woman of twenty-eight, Lily was unmarried.

War came. Caroline and John still had four sons, and all enlisted. Much to my surprise I found that two of them, Leslie and Colin, had moved to Queensland and were living in Gordonvale, a sugar-growing town near Cairns, when they signed up in August 1914, only weeks after war was declared. Both were at the Gallipoli landing on 25 April 1915. Colin went missing that day, but his death was only confirmed for his parents eighteen months later. Leslie survived Gallipoli but was killed in France in August 1916. Neither man's remains were ever found; the men are commemorated on memorials at Lone Pine, on Gallipoli, and at Villers-Bretonneux.

Their younger brother, Alan, enlisted from Tasmania in March 1915 and managed to have himself transferred to the same battalion as his brothers, presumably to be closer to them. After a few months on Gallipoli he joined the fighting in France. After Leslie's death, Alan requested and was granted a compassionate discharge from the army on the grounds that his parents had lost two sons and were partly dependent on him as the only son left. He arrived home in Liffey in November 1916.

But here's the twist. Alan had not told the truth. He was not, in fact, the last surviving brother because all along his oldest brother, Walter, had been living in Bracknell with his wife and four children. Walter did eventually enlist, in late 1917, and made it to France just before the Armistice, when it was too late for him to see much action. He returned to Tasmania unscathed in October 1919, took up a soldier-settlement block near Longford, and had four more children.

* * *

You can learn a great deal from archival records and local newspapers, and that is how I put this story together. And yet there are limits. Often you can uncover "what happened" – or some of it – but not "why". The emotional coherence that once held people's decisions together is lost.

For instance, Leslie and Colin had left Tasmania before the war to strike out in Queensland. Why? Was there a family argument? Perhaps they were looking for work (which is why most young people leave Tasmania, as I know myself), or perhaps they just wanted to get out of this remote, tight-knit community where everyone seemed to be related to everyone else. But why travel so far, to a place so different?

And then there is young Alan, a troubled soul. He rushed to the war when, at age twenty, he still needed parental permission to enlist, but after his brothers died he lied his way out of the army to get back home again. Did his family connive at this? Given how long it took for letters to travel between continents, I suspect he had no opportunity to share his plans with them.

Clearly this was a family in acute emotional distress. How did Alan explain his arrival back in Liffey? What was said around the kitchen table at Silverburn in late 1916? None of us can suggest Alan was a coward. We weren't there. But the fact that no-one in authority checked his story (for example, by requesting information from the local police) suggests that Alan may not have been an effective soldier, and that the army was willing to quietly let him go. Did his older brother Walter know of Alan's lies? If so, it must have placed Walter in a most dreadful position. Perhaps – here's a thought – his enlistment was his way of making reparation for Alan's duplicity.

The postwar years brought fresh worry for Caroline and John. In 1921 their oldest daughter, Beryl, died, leaving her own three children to Caroline and John to care for. Alan married and had a daughter but in the mid-1920s, restless as ever, he moved with his family to Queensland, to Gordonvale, where his brothers had lived before the war. I tried hard but I never discovered whatever it was that lured the Saunders men to this particular town so far away. Alan died there in 1930 of war-related illness, according to death notices inserted by his family in the Gordonvale newspaper. He was only thirty-five.

Caroline Saunders died in 1926 aged sixty-two. When John died in 1937, aged seventy-nine, he had been predeceased by his wife and seven of his ten children. The remaining three buried their parents next to their sister Beryl under a single headstone at Mountain Vale. They added the names of their solider brothers – Leslie, Colin and Alan – who had died "For King and Country". Thus were these adventurous, impetuous boys brought home – symbolically – to join their family.

* * *

Social historians of the First World War invariably point out that bereavement in war – the scale of it, the shock of it, and the fact that relatives could not be present at the death or bury their dead with traditional rites – was not the same as in peacetime. It isn't natural that adult children should die before their parents. All true. And yet if we go back before 1914, we discover that many people were already in mourning when the war broke out. Each of my two Saunders couples in Liffey lost three children before 1914, and that can hardly have been a unique experience.

And so to Maria and William Saunders. They married in 1886 and also established a farm in Liffey, where they had eleven children. In 1901, diphtheria broke out among children in the district. This bacterial infection, transmitted by coughing and sneezing, was made worse in small houses where children shared cots and beds. It attacks the respiratory system; if unchecked, a toxin creates a thick grey film in the nose and throat. Many victims who die are unable to breathe.

In the space of a week in October 1901, Maria and William watched three of their children die in this way: Stanley, aged nineteen months; Horace, thirteen years; and finally baby Grace, only a few months old. All three received separate funerals at Mountain Vale. Three times, a procession set out from the Saunders' house to travel a few kilometres on foot, surrounded by forest, behind a horse-drawn hearse to the little wooden church at Mountain Vale. Nothing marks their graves now.

Not surprisingly, Maria and William sold up and moved. They had more children, and were living in Hadspen, near Launceston, when war came. Two sons who might have volunteered had already died, but they still had three eligible sons, Harold (known as Errol) and twins Lawrence and Clarence. These young men would have had plenty of friends who rushed to the colours – including their own Saunders cousins – and yet they hesitated.

Many did, tied to home by family obligations or work on family farms and businesses. For those who stayed, it must have taken a particular sort of courage to accept that their lot would be to plant potatoes, mend fences and get the harvest in; that they would be shooting rabbits and possums, not the beastly Hun. Under the weight of all this, only Lawrence went. He enlisted in October 1916 and served on the

Western Front until he was killed in action in Belgium in February 1918. He is buried in a cemetery near Ypres. His twin brother Clarence stayed home, married and had a family, living a long and outwardly uneventful life.

There are tales aplenty of twins who enlisted, fought and died together, but these two didn't. How did they decide who would stay and who would go? Could it possibly have come down to the toss of a coin?

* * *

The more we attempt to dwell inside the lives of people in the past, especially ordinary people who leave little trace of themselves in the historical record, the more questions we uncover that elude easy answers. So be it. My stories from Liffey are fragmented and unresolved. But small stories inspired by encounters with local places often ask us to reconsider broader national narratives: Anzac, or something else that we cherish. They nibble away at accepted versions of history and propose new relationships between apparently disparate experiences.

Who is a hero and who is a coward? Who is remembered and who is forgotten? How is the memory of the dead to be preserved? That man with a gun – that man with a spear – is he a patriot or is he a criminal? These binary questions are not useful. What is important is that we are attentive to whatever unquiet stories the land might reveal.

Rock, Water, Paper

In March 2023 the Australian War Memorial invited Canberra schoolchildren to name the two enormous cranes then hovering over the Memorial's building extensions. The cranes were henceforward to be named "Duffy", for one of Simpson's donkeys, and "Teddy", after Edward Sheean, Australia's latest Victoria Cross recipient. "Poppy", "Anzac" and "Biscuit" were among the names rejected.

The exercise was presumably designed to make Canberrans feel good about the controversial $550 million project. Cranes hovering overhead and massive earthworks front and rear were inviting many uneasy glances at a building that has nestled for decades at the foot of Mount Ainslie as if it grew of its own accord out of the ancient earth.

Of course it did not. As Michael McKernan showed in his history of the Memorial, *Here Is Their Spirit* (1991), between the official announcement of the site in 1923 and the opening of the building by prime minister John Curtin in 1941, hurdles and setbacks tested the faith of the Memorial's most ardent supporters. Even in 1941 the building was incomplete: the exhibition galleries were opened to the public but the grounds and commemorative areas, including the Roll of Honour and the Hall of Memory, took several more decades to finish.

All those struggles might be forgotten, but the project was once regarded with such trepidation by federal authorities that it was held to a budget – £250,000 – that was manifestly inadequate even for the modest, restrained building that Charles Bean, one of the Memorial's founders, had dreamed of. He had imagined it on a hilltop: "still, beautiful, gleaming white and silent". Politicians, though, were more interested in memorials in their local districts than a national memorial most of their constituents would never see. After a vexed and abortive architectural competition, a design for the national memorial was agreed upon in 1929, but with the onset of the Depression the project had to be shelved. Finally, in February 1934, the building contract was awarded to Simmie & Co., a firm that built many of Canberra's early public and commercial buildings.

It's long been a fancy of mine that the land itself tried to reject the building being raised upon it, calling up malevolent spirits to cast spells over it. For starters, the winter of 1934 was the wettest then on record. Next, the foundations took much longer to excavate than expected because the trial holes dug during the tender period had not revealed how hard and rocky the site really was. Quizzed over delays in the project, Simmie's principals complained that they had been "grossly misled" in this regard.

Eventually in November 1935 the building was declared weathertight and ready for occupation, but after all that effort the result – a long, low construction of garish red bricks from the local brickworks – was embarrassingly basic. The beautiful Hawkesbury sandstone cladding that lends so much quiet beauty to the building had not yet been applied, and influential observers complained it looked "squat" and "prison-like". Building plans were hastily altered to raise the height of the walls and later the dome, causing more headaches for Simmie.

Despite these inauspicious circumstances, a doughty bunch of about twenty-five staff began preparing to move themselves and their families from Melbourne to the infant capital, along with 770 tons of objects, paintings, photographs, books, archival records and stores. These had been stored and exhibited in leased premises in Sydney and Melbourne.

The Australian War Memorial under construction, 1940
Photographer: Richard Strangman
Australian War Memorial XS0120

In late 1935 deputy director Tasman "Tas" Heyes moved into a house in Forrest, south of the Molonglo river, but director John Treloar made what he called a "private arrangement". After several previous stints living in Canberra, his wife, Clarissa, had refused to move this time and remained in Melbourne with their four school-age children. Treloar set himself up in the Memorial with his suitcases, a wardrobe and a single stretcher. He was not a man with elaborate personal wants; as a staff clerk on Gallipoli in 1915, Treloar had slept and worked in the same dugout and took advantage of the short commute to work punishing hours. This he proceeded to do again. Although not a cold or humourless man, austerity suited him.

* * *

It had been a wet weekend, and from his house in Forrest late on Sunday afternoon, 12 January 1936, Tas Heyes was keeping an uneasy eye on the sky. In those near-treeless days you could see far across Canberra, and it was obvious that a storm was gathering over Mount Ainslie. He and Treloar had inspected the Memorial building on the previous Friday evening after heavy rain and found water seeping in through an unfaced brick wall on the lower-ground floor where the library would be. Cases of collection material stood nearby, ready for shelving. The water seepage had not been serious then, but now, when Heyes found that the storm had blotted out all sight of the Memorial from his home, he got into his car.

Those malign spirits had decided as a final angry gesture to turn on one of Canberra's cataclysmic summer storms. Today, staff in Canberra's cultural institutions fully comprehend the power of these events, but in 1936 the Memorial's building was piteously vulnerable and the newly arrived Melburnians were quite innocent of the harsh extremes and occasional violence of the weather on the high plains south of the Brindabellas.

Mount Ainslie was the centre of a terrific cloudburst, and from its slopes torrents of water were descending. As Heyes struggled across in his car, Treloar was already there, dealing with the crisis with the help of the building's two watchmen, Thomas Aldridge and George Wells, at their change of shift. The stormwater drain on Mount Ainslie's lower slopes had overflowed and water was washing silt and debris down to the suburbs of Ainslie, Reid and Braddon, and becoming trapped in the excavation around the Memorial building. The lower-ground floor was below the watercourse and water was advancing into the building, sweeping down passages and up to the cases containing precious war records.

Many of the cases were raised from the floor on timber baulks, but this precaution had ceased when the building had been declared weathertight, and now several hundred cases were in immediate danger. The three men on site needed help, but none of the staff at that time had home telephones, so Aldridge drove off to gather them from their homes, leaving Treloar and Wells to scavenge timber to make platforms for the cases.

Scarcely had they begun this task when Aldridge returned, having abandoned his car where it had become bogged even before he got out of the grounds. By now, more water was sweeping into the building

John Treloar, 1941
Photographer: Edward Cranstone
Australian War Memorial 005915

across a landing that had been built at a rear entrance to help bring in large objects. Treloar and Aldridge tried to dig a ditch to divert the water, but, as Treloar later reported, "the rocky ground defied the shovels which were the only tools we had". They tried to wreck the landing but it was too well built.

Leaving his men to struggle with the records cases, Treloar phoned the fire brigade and was told that the chief fire officer could send men to pump water out of the building but only if it reached six inches, and they could not help move records or exhibits. Soon after, the telephone service broke down, leaving the three drenched and desperate men isolated. At this point, Tas Heyes finally made it through.

It was growing dark and the building in its primitive state had hardly any lights. Water was washing under doors and through unfinished sections of the roof. The waste pipes of wash basins and drinking fountains, as Treloar reported later, "threw into the air jets of water several feet high". Water was about to enter the room where the works of art were stored. It was impossible to move the cases in time, and improvised squeegees proved to be hopeless. Using chisels and their bare hands, Treloar and his staff tore up the floorboards at the entrance to the room, and the water, which was now creeping around the edges of the art cases, escaped beneath the building. Heyes set out in his car in another attempt to round up more staff to help; by 8 p.m. about a dozen men were on the site and a few oil lamps had been obtained.

The worst was over. Manholes over drains were opened and water swept into them. Staff continued to clear the building of as much water as was possible, working in the dark with only improvised tools. By 1 a.m. Treloar decided to suspend work. The men were exhausted and most had been wet through for hours.

Treloar later told a colleague that the suit he had been wearing that day was ruined, a rare reference to himself and his personal comfort. Where he slept for the rest of that night isn't known, but Heyes, a friend and colleague for many years, probably took him back to his house. Forrest had received no more than an ordinary shower of rain.

* * *

The next day the *Canberra Times* carried long reports of the flood. Six inches (more than 150 millimetres) of rain had fallen on Civic and the inner north in ninety-five minutes. The paper had rarely had such a dramatic local event to cover. The Memorial's misfortunes were ignored at first in favour of the dramatic rescue of motorists stranded on Constitution Avenue, the many roads that were scoured or washed away, the five feet of water in the basement of Beauchamp House (a hotel in Acton), the "pitiful" state of Miss Mabbott's frock shop in Civic, and the washed-out gardens and drowned chickens in Ainslie. These local calamities mattered more than what had happened at the Memorial, about which the paper finally gave a brief report the next day. Few people really knew what went on in this strange new building anyway.

Monday, 13 January at the Memorial was a heavy, depressing day of mopping up, opening hundreds of cases and separating the wet from the dry. Two to three inches of water had entered the building. Some 2648 books were damaged and 719 had to be rebound. Among the most valuable was a large collection of histories of First World War German military units, which Treloar described to a newspaper reporter as "irreplaceable". More than 700 cases of archival records were damaged, as were 10,327 photographic negatives. Thankfully, paintings had been stored on their edges in crates so that only the frames were soiled, but 389 were damaged and 300 had to be remounted.

In the end, the damage was not so bad. The museum objects, stored on the upper floor, were untouched. Some of the damaged records were duplicates and, as Treloar reassured his board of management, water-stained books would not be less valuable as records, and the pictures when remounted would be "as attractive as formerly".

Prints existed of some of the negatives, and the emulsified surfaces of the negatives had fortunately been fitted with cover glasses to protect them. Most of the records cases had been stored on timber two or three inches above the floor, although Treloar bitterly regretted his decision to abandon this practice shortly before the flood.

The salvage operation was instructive and useful in many ways. Treloar was enormously capable, but he liked to consult experts and tried to keep himself abreast of practices in museums, galleries and libraries in Australia and overseas. Here was a chance to call in some help and renew important associations. Leslie Bowles, a sculptor who often worked with the Memorial, travelled from Melbourne to advise on the treatment of some battlefield models affected by the flood. Although Kodak and the Council for Scientific and Industrial Research were contacted for advice on the treatment of the negatives, Treloar soon turned to an expert from the photographic branch of the Department of Commerce in Melbourne.

The paper items needed the most treatment. A hot-air blower was obtained for the soaked documents, and eight local teenage girls arrived with their mothers' electric irons on the Thursday after the flood. Treloar had been informed that the best way to fully dry and flatten the documents, newspapers and pages of books was to iron them, presumably with a piece of cloth over the paper. This was to be the job for the next few weeks for Enid, Ivy, Agnes, Betty, Jean, Thelma, Stella and Gwen, girls recruited through the Canberra YWCA. Its secretary had had many applications for the curious engagement. The girls were paid under the award for government-employed servants and laundresses, but surely never was a laundress entrusted with such a strange and delicate task. How anxiously Treloar must have hovered about, watching them at their work.

Some of the damp documents were part of the Memorial's collection of unit war diaries – not soldiers' private diaries (although the Memorial had a fine collection of those as well) but official records kept by each military unit. For Treloar, they were probably the most important part of the collection and he knew them intimately. They were mostly created on the battlefront, and it would have been agonising to imagine them engulfed by muddy water in the very building created to house and protect them in perpetuity.

Support and commiserations poured in. Arthur Bazley, assistant to official historian Charles Bean, phoned Treloar from Sydney to offer any help he could, using his Sydney contacts. Bean, on holiday in Austinmer, wrote to Treloar that he and Heyes "must have this comfort, that you know that all concerned are so aware of your carefulness and forethought, that their only feeling will be one of sympathy". Federal interior minister Thomas Paterson, who had responsibility for the Memorial, telephoned to find Treloar still lamenting the cases stacked directly on the floor. His kindly advice: "an officer could not expect to be a prophet".

* * *

After all the years of work and worry, Treloar was not present at the opening of the Memorial on Armistice Day, 1941. He was in uniform again, based in Cairo managing the collecting effort for yet another war, leaving Tas Heyes to organise the ceremony.

The first Anzac Day at the Memorial was held in 1942, the national ceremony having previously been held at Parliament House. With so many Australians fighting abroad and the enemy at the nation's doorstep, Anzac Day in the nation's capital had never been so sombre (and wouldn't be again until 2020, when Covid restrictions forced the cancellation of traditional commemorations).

No veterans' march was held that year, and Anzac Day sports were cancelled. The *Canberra Times* editorialised that the day found Australia a "battle station". Anzacs "now stood guard on their own land" and any honour owed them was never so much due as on that day. It was to be a day "not of works but abiding faith".

At the Memorial a twenty-minute ceremony held in the commemorative courtyard was attended by a mere 600 people. Around them were bare walls: no Roll of Honour yet, and an empty Hall of Memory. A single aircraft flew low overhead. Weatherwise, the morning was cool and overcast, but there was no rain.

What Did *You* Do in the War, Sandy?

The death of Barry Humphries in April 2023 brought forth abundant reminders of his remarkable and diverse talents and achievements. Actor, writer, poet, artist, bibliophile: Humphries was a gift to obituarists because he was rarely out of the limelight, either as himself or acting out parts of himself in the many personae he created.

But while others were revelling in their favourite memories of Edna Everage, Les Patterson or Barry McKenzie, I took myself off in a different, quieter direction: to 36 Gallipoli Crescent, in fact, a street fictitiously located in the real Melbourne suburb of Glen Iris. This was the home of Sandy Stone, the most subtly drawn of all Humphries's characters. I had no strife finding a "pozzie for the vehicle", as Sandy often said of his own parking misadventures, because comparatively few people remember this boring old beggar (a polite euphemism for bugger in Sandy's day) of the suburbs.

Humphries, born in 1934, grew up in nearby Camberwell, where his father became a prosperous master builder. Eric Humphries built three houses for his family in Christowel Street, numbers 30, 38 and 36; the last was where they settled for good in 1937. Sandy and Beryl Stone's imaginary house at 36 Gallipoli Crescent was "built" on these memories, although whether the style was mock Tudor, mock Elizabethan, neo-Georgian, Spanish mission or Californian bungalow Sandy doesn't say. Eric Humphries could build them all. There was a driveway for the vehicle, a shady porch, and a tradesman's hatch at the side. Sandy and Beryl called the house "Kia Ora", a Māori phrase for "hello".

The Stones' life together began just as the Depression was easing. On Sunday afternoons, while Kia Ora was being built, they would come and sit on the joists with a thermos and a pile of *Australian Home Beautifuls*. It's never clear what sort of job Sandy had, but the couple were comfortably off and could afford the sorts of conveniences much prized by Humphries's desperately aspirational parents. The Stones had an electric refrigerator instead of an ice box, an electric stove and oven instead of an Early Kooka, and an indoor toilet instead of an outdoor dunny covered in morning glory.

In Sandy and Beryl's garden there were "rhodies" and "hyderanges" (rhododendrons and hydrangeas), a silver birch and maybe a "jaca" (jacaranda), but probably no roses (Humphries's mother thought them "a bit old-fashioned"), and certainly no shaggy eucalypts. Eucalypts, as well as paling fences, chicken coops and any structure with a corrugated iron roof, were considered emblems of the working-class existence Humphries's parents had managed to escape. After their wedding, Eric and Louisa Humphries had moved to Camberwell from the less respectable suburb of Thornbury, but, as it turned out, only a bluestone lane separated the houses in Christowel Street from a remnant pocket of poverty in old Camberwell.

"We stared at each other sometimes, the poor and I," Humphries later remembered, young Barry on a ladder propped against the back fence, and the poor children, with their bloodied knees and runny noses, staring back from their derelict backyards.

* * *

The Sandy Stone monologues were written either for sound recordings or as the "adagio act" in Humphries's live touring shows. He published the collected scripts in 1990 under the title *The Life and Death of Sandy Stone*, edited by his friend Collin O'Brien. A television series of the same name was broadcast that year by the ABC, recorded in front of a studio audience whom Sandy addresses from his patterned velvet armchair. He is always styled as a middle-aged-to-elderly man, in a dressing-gown and slippers, cradling a hot water bottle.

Often Sandy pauses an anecdote to note with deep approval that someone was a "returned man", once a common term for someone who had fought abroad in one or both of the world wars. There was his friend Pat Hennessy, who'd recently had occasion to bury his wife and who was so lost without her that in three years he'd not cleaned the S-bend in his toilet. He was a returned man. So was their local postie, and so was the specialist who broke the news to Sandy and Beryl that they could never have children. As for the vestryman up at Holy Trinity church whose son was a hippie: although not actually a returned man, he was "one of the nicest people you could ever wish to meet".

My parents and I never missed an episode of the ABC series, and my father delighted to imitate the exact note of serene reverence in Sandy's voice when referring to a "returned man". Dad's father, George, really had been a returned man, a quiet sort of chappie, Sandy would have said, and to look at George nobody would have thought he'd been a prankster and a scallywag before enlistment. After service on Gallipoli and Pozières he returned silent and deeply introverted, happy to accept an office job and a peaceful life in the suburbs. But he did retain the impish sense of humour that has become a family trait, hence my father's rich appreciation of Sandy Stone.

With Barry Humphries's death I thought back to those evenings in front of the telly with my parents and became curious about Sandy's actual returned status. I found it surprisingly ambiguous. Sandy is a regular at his local RSL, and when he needs to have a surgical operation – a "little op" – he is entitled to have it done at "the Repat", which as his Melbourne audiences would have known was the Repatriation General Hospital in Heidelberg. (The term "repatriation" in this context has fallen into disuse but was once a uniquely Australian descriptor for the return of Australian men and women after war service, and their further support through pensions and benefits.)

Sandy has obviously served in some capacity, but what? He first appeared in 1958 in a sound recording, "Days of the Week", written as the B-side for a 45-rpm record. (Mrs Everage took the A-side.) Also in 1958 Humphries published a short story titled "Sandy Stone's Big Week" in the Canberra student magazine *Prometheus*. Nothing happens in Sandy's "big week". A pot-bellied Sandy is discovered in his garden in the early evening, watering his shrubs. As the light dims, all that is visible of him is his white shirt "and the white arc of water from his garden hose". Called inside by Beryl, he goes in, switches on the wireless, seats himself in the patterned velvet armchair, rolls a cigarette (later he is a non-smoker) and thinks about the events of the coming week. The highlight will be an RSL meeting on the Friday night at Gallipoli Hall. That's it.

Nothing much ever does happen to this emasculated Anzac. He makes a trip back to Gallipoli in 1968 with a group of cobbers and a Turkish guide (who spoke "perfect Australian") and writes a painfully dull letter from the "Istanbul Hilton" to Beryl about the few hours they'd spent stumbling around the peninsula getting souvenir snaps. Perhaps this monologue was prompted by historian Ken Inglis's reports for the *Canberra Times* of the 1965 RSL pilgrimage to Gallipoli, but Humphries ultimately rejected the idea of making Sandy a First World War man, and this piece, "Anzac Sandy", was never performed.

Instead, the Second World War became Sandy's war, although, as Humphries himself admitted, Sandy's military status was still nebulous. The development of the character coincided with growing scepticism among some Australians, bordering on hostility, towards all things Anzac in the 1960s, but Humphries avoided using Sandy as a vehicle for the kind of biting critique that Alan Seymour explored in his play *The One Day of the Year*, first performed in 1960. Nor was Sandy a violent, war-damaged tyrant like the father in George Johnston's *My Brother Jack* (1964). And again, Humphries was uninterested in the public debate over the system of repatriation that was satirised in John Whiting's polemical novel *Be in It, Mate!* (1969).

Sandy was never about any of that. The point of Sandy was to be boring. His creator's declared aim was to see how far he could bore audiences before they rose up in revolt. Acknowledging the influence of Samuel Beckett and the avant-garde art movement known as dadaism, with its explorations of nonsense and irrationality, Humphries wanted not to please his audiences but to provoke and shock. Gradually he alighted on the idea of boredom as the way to do it and, turning inwards, found all the material he needed within the suburban wasteland, as he saw it, of his youth.

Hence Sandy's maddening, circumlocutory monologues punctuated by pointless pauses, digressions and repetitions. His attention will get snagged on a point of inconsequential detail and audiences watch, transfixed, as he struggles to free himself. This, for instance, from "Shades of Sandy" (1981):

> Little Gwennie's husband, Jack, went to his Reward about two years ago. Yes, it would be two years since Jack went to his Reward. It would be a good two years. It would be all of a good two years.

Also in that monologue is Sandy's immortal critique of the domestic pop-up toaster, specifically the Morphy Richards model that threw Beryl across the room one day when she tried to dig a crumpet out with a fork. No matter the brand of toaster, the crumpet is never taken into account. "You slip one in and half an hour later, if you are lucky, it glides to the surface, as white as a lily." But sometimes the opposite happens:

> Flames leap out of the toaster. You've got to bash it underneath with a broomstick, and then you're on the kitchen floor trying to find it, and over the sink, scraping off the black fur till there's nothing left but a couple of crumpet holes. A black crumpet hole is no use to man nor beast.

There is a little knob on the side of the toaster, Sandy continues, to indicate light to dark. Easy to miss. Beryl missed it for years and then, when she found it, she couldn't leave it alone. But the interesting thing, he concludes, is that *"it's not connected to anything"* (Sandy's emphasis). "It's got a mind of its own."

* * *

Ruminating in 1990 on the origins of Sandy, Humphries recalled how, after having dropped out of university, he succumbed to parental pressure and took a "real" job in the city with the EMI record label. On his morning commute, always running late, he often met his neighbour Mr Whittle, a childless man of his parents' age who would invariably greet young Barry with "a polite and old-fashioned little squeeze" of his grey trilby hat. For Humphries, this man came to epitomise not just his parents' generation, but "Respectability Itself": punctuality, industry, courtesy, thrift, temperance, niceness. "I despised him."

In 1956, desperate to escape, Humphries got married and snatched an acting job in Sydney. He was unhappy there too, especially in the depressing old boarding house near Centennial Park where he and his wife Brenda were staying. Breakfast was had in a shared kitchen with other tenants, mostly aged and itinerant men, all lonely. Walking along Bondi Beach one blustery winter's afternoon, Humphries encountered a wiry old fellow of about sixty-five with thin sandy hair, finely capillaried cheeks, a two-tone cardigan and "freckled, marsupial paws". When Humphries asked the time, he was told: "Approximately in the vicinity of half past five."

In that moment, he had the last pieces in place to create Sandy Stone, including the sibilant "S's" caused by ill-fitting dentures, and the thin, dry voice Humphries recognised as "the antithesis of the rugged Australian stereotype".

What unified these men in Humphries's mind, I think, was not their ex-digger status but his perception of them as lonely, ageing men. Confused and anxious about his future, perhaps his greatest fear was that he would end up like them. True, Mr Whittle did wear a returned serviceman's badge on his lapel, but Humphries was careful not to overplay that. Sandy could not be a war bore because he would have had to bore audiences on subjects about which Humphries knew little. Instead, he turned to a subject on which he really was an expert, life in the Australian suburbs. To express his rage and frustration at the tedium imposed upon him in his youth, he needed a technique that would be, he said, "monumentally, grindingly prosaic".

* * *

The most interesting event in Sandy's life is his death, which occurs in his sleep while Beryl is absent on the *Women's Weekly* World Discovery Tour that she had been hankering to do for years. Death frees him to return as a ghost.

He enjoys watching his own funeral and the wake afterwards back at Kia Ora. He watches as Beryl puts the house up for sale and disposes of his effects, assisted by their neighbour Clarrie Lockwood from 43 Gallipoli Crescent. Clarrie heaves Sandy's armchair into his Vanguard ute, along with various other bygones of Sandy and Beryl's life together, and takes them to the Holy Trinity opportunity shop. It is obvious to everyone except Sandy that Beryl is more gleeful than grief-stricken, and after the house sells she moves to Queensland, where she and Clarrie later marry.

Kia Ora is bought by Mr and Mrs Cosmopolis, "a delightful multicultural ethnic minority Greek couple", who are expecting a baby. Mrs Cosmopolis notices Sandy's armchair in the op shop and buys it, and so, in Sandy's final monologue, "Sandy Comes Home" (1985), we find him back at 36 Gallipoli Crescent, still in his old armchair, watching his house being renovated.

This monologue cracks open the racism that Sandy has been putting down in layers since the 1930s, when fruit and vegetables were delivered to Kia Ora through the tradesman's hatch by the "yellow hand" of the "little smiling Chinaman", Charlie O'Hoy. Sandy could bestow a tolerant glow over Charlie, and the Greek couple who operated the local fish and chip shop, and even the Angelo brothers, Italians who as terrazzo specialists did most of the porches in the street. But when in 1938 an "Israelite" couple named Eckstein moved into the first block of flats in Glen Iris: they were the "thin end of the wedge" as far as Sandy was concerned. They opened the floodgates and then it was "Come One, Come All".

The Stubbings' beautiful home at number 52, for instance, was bought recently and remodelled by a Vietnamese couple called Ng. That's their name, Sandy tells us, incredulous, and "you could smell their cooking on the bowling green". Number 37, the home of Vi and Alan Chapman, was bought by Bruno Agostino and his family of eleven.

> Once they moved in, that once-lovely home was swarming with dagos night and day. Talk about build. They built on the back, they built on the front, they built on the left, they built on the right... they built a balustrade right across the front of the home, with fountains and statues and lions everywhere. It was like a cement safari.

The Agostinos dug up all of Vi's *"magnificent"* garden, including the pin oak Vi bought as a seedling years before from the Methodist Church fete. It resisted the bulldozer for the best part of a day, until the "Eye-ties" got a block and tackle to it and finally it came down "with a groan you could hear up and down the crescent".

Only as they chopped it up did the Agostinos discover a bit of rotten wood nailed onto one of the branches, which was all that was left of the treehouse little Neil Chapman had played in before the war.

> Of course, little Neil was beheaded in Borneo. Some Jap with a sword said "Neil!" [kneel] and he did, and that was that. It's terrible to think that your destiny can be in your own name.

Without a pause Sandy rambles on remorselessly, as he always does. The monologue ends with Mrs Cosmopolis bustling in to clear away the last of the things that Beryl hadn't bothered with, including Beryl and Sandy's wedding photo and a lock of his mother's hair, which he'd been keeping in a cigarette tin. They go into the rubbish.

* * *

"Sandy Comes Home" appears to be the last Sandy monologue Humphries wrote, and it was the longest. By then audiences had developed a certain affectionate sympathy for Sandy, which made his racism even more shocking. Humphries always enjoyed the deep hush that greeted Sandy's anti-Semitism. "Perhaps," he mused in 1990, "we had not until then fully apprehended that we, who had invented Niceness, could also be very nicely anti-Semitic. It was a salutary discovery."

Sandy's ex-service status was just a device to tie him to the past and associate him with the most conservative element in Australia at the time, the RSL. The young Barry Humphries had spotted a much older man – his neighbour Mr Whittle – and despised him for his "respectability". For comedic purposes he was uninterested in the idea that people of Mr Whittle's generation had lived through and suffered much. But after two economic depressions (1890s and 1930s), two world wars and a cold war, small wonder that they took refuge in suburban routine and hard-won material comforts. Humphries himself became rusted on to his long-held desire to shock, and over many years must have developed an ability to avert his gaze from the real pain he could inflict. Transphobic comments made in 2016 and 2018 seem to bear this out.

A word about Mr Whittle. Kenneth Roy Whittle was born in 1897, trained as a surveyor and became a public servant. He and his wife, Alice, moved into 42 Christowel Street, Camberwell in the early 1930s. He was not an ex-serviceman; there is no evidence he enlisted or attempted to enlist in either world war. Nor were the Whittles childless. Their only child, June Elizabeth, died in 1933, aged two, the year before Barry was born. Had she lived, they might have been playmates.

From a Distance

In April 2024, with Anzac Day approaching, I got to thinking that it was then ten years since the beginning of the much-anticipated centenary of Anzac: those four long years of commercial and state-sponsored events and projects marking 100 years since Australia's involvement in the First World War.

Peak Anzac was reached, in my recollection at least, between November 2014 and April 2015. The bracketing events commemorated the departure of the first convoy of Australian troops from Albany in Western Australia in November 1914, and the landing at Gallipoli on 25 April 1915. An estimated 8000 Australians and 2000 New Zealanders travelled to Gallipoli that April for services there, while in Canberra 120,000 people attended the national dawn service at the Australian War Memorial.

Things then simmered down considerably, and by November 2018 much of the Anzac energy had drained away – though not before an extraordinary amount of money had been spent. The following year, when historian Carolyn Holbrook attempted to make sense of what had just happened, she offered some figures drawn from work done in mid-2015 by Anzac commentator David Stephens. Germany's projected commemorative spend for each soldier and civilian killed in the war was $2. France was committed to spending $52, the United Kingdom $109. Australia? A projected spend of $8889 per soldier and civilian killed. My lord.

The first couple of years of the centenary saw an exhausting round of ceremonies, events, exhibitions, art commissions, television documentaries and websites; everyone was trying to out-Anzac everyone else. Some of these were clearly devised to offer people a chance to experience and share heightened emotions in a safe way. The Anzac Days that many of us have grown up with have always done that, of course, but this was next level. The most obvious example was a cluster of events in Australia and New Zealand called "Camp Gallipoli", whereby people paid to join others for an evening under the stars to remember the Gallipoli landings. Attendees at the Tasmanian event on 24 April 2015 were promised an "emotional roller coaster" where they could "sing, eat, drink, laugh (and cry) but most importantly ... be together".

There were some epic embarrassments. The commemorative television features sometimes rated poorly, and the Camp Gallipoli Foundation found itself stripped of its charitable status for having failed to pass on profits to veterans' charities (claims it rejected). Anything that smacks of commercial exploitation of Anzac has always attracted suspicion, and the limits of tolerance were breached by supermarket chain Woolworths just before Anzac Day 2015, when a public outcry forced the cancellation of a digital advertising campaign inviting users to upload an image of an Anzac to a picture generator. The generator added the green Woolies logo and the words "Fresh in our Memories".

Among the sugar-rush projects, however, many initiatives were of enduring value, especially from libraries, archives and museums keen to use the opportunity to exhibit and digitise objects and records from their collections. I was involved in one or two, or three – no, four – of these, and they certainly did reveal hitherto unseen material and nuanced stories at a time when the public appetite was extraordinarily high. But I too became overwhelmed by so many stories, so many young men's (and occasionally women's) faces, and so many sad artefacts reminding us of all that loss of life and potential.

From a distance, these stories all seem the same. You need to get up close to discern the differences, but by 2018 my vision was blurred, my emotions were numb and my capacity for surprise was gone. It had also been such a noisy time. Anzac and Remembrance Days always end with a minute's silence (it used to be two minutes) but there was not much silence during the four years of the Anzac centenary. Only gradually did my ears stop ringing long enough for me to lean into the post-centenary silence. By then hardly anyone was bothering any more. I was like American poet Mary Oliver sitting on her old stone bench in a forest, listening to the silence. "What's magical, sometimes, has deeper roots than reason," says the poet. I doubt she was thinking of historical research when she wrote that, but there *are* some stories that take you deeper than reason, and they can still be found if you sit quietly long enough.

* * *

In April 2024 I found one of these in the small town of Uralla, twenty-three kilometres southwest of Armidale on the New South Wales tablelands. Upstairs in McCrossin's Mill Museum (the local museum, named because it is housed in a former flour mill) is a display about Cecil Stoker, a Uralla man who enlisted for the First World War in July 1915 and was killed in France less than a year later, after barely two weeks at the front, in June 1916. This story is best told backwards.

In 1982, by their own account, two members of the museum committee were inspecting the interior of Uralla's oldest existing building when they noticed a boarded-up fireplace. The building in Bridge Street was a former general store known as Stoker's Store, empty and earmarked for demolition. They knew that technically they were trespassing, but "boys being boys", and it being a Sunday afternoon when there was "nothing else to do", they tore the timber away.

Inside, covered in soot and rubbish, was a rusty tin trunk, and inside *that* was another trunk in pristine condition. Inside that second trunk – which they opened without hesitation – they discovered Stoker family memorabilia from 1860 to 1951, including many artefacts, photographs and letters related to the military service and death of

Cecil Stoker. Their surmise was that Stoker's mother, Elizabeth Stoker, had sealed up all the things in 1951 and had them hidden away. She died in 1954 aged eighty.

Back home in front of my computer in Canberra, I established that Elizabeth had made her will in 1951, so it does indeed seem she made final decisions then about what to do with her possessions. After her death her estate was duly dealt with by her two surviving sons, but the trunk mustn't have been mentioned in her will. Her sons presumably didn't know or had forgotten about it, and there it remained until two young Indiana Joneses broke into it in 1982.

Private Cecil Stoker, 1916
Australian War Memorial, H05845

Cecil Stoker was a junior railway porter in 1915, aged just seventeen, when he put his age up to eighteen so he could enlist. His father had died in 1910, when Cecil was twelve, leaving his mother to run the business and raise three sons on her own. He was obviously hell-bent on going to the war; he and nearly all the other men in the Uralla Football Club enlisted together.

From a distance, this is the type of story upon which the Anzac legend is built. If we wonder why that legend is so powerful, we need look no further than this. A beautiful young man leaves his family and his rural hometown to fling his life away in a global conflict not of his making. His family is shattered by grief, but his community honours him for upholding values of courage and sacrifice and later cherishes his story in the local museum. The Stoker display at the McCrossin's Mill Museum in Uralla is a micro-version of the Australian War Memorial in Canberra, shrunk to fit. There is even a spray of preserved flowers brought back from Stoker's grave after someone from Uralla visited in 1992.

The most remarkable thing about the Stoker story is the completeness of the family archive Elizabeth kept. The memorabilia goes back to their earliest days in Uralla and includes a photograph of their shop when it was a tinsmith operated by Cecil's grandfather. There is a family photograph of Elizabeth and William Stoker and their three young sons, and a memorial card printed after William's death. There is a snap of the dozen or so young men from Uralla who enlisted together, proudly posed around a motor car, still in their civvies, and a portrait photograph of Cecil in uniform taken at a studio in Armidale. There's a birthday card from his "special friend" Vida Williamson, a local Uralla girl, wishing him bon voyage. There's a postcard Cecil sent to his mother from his troopship HMAT *Warilda*, and a photograph of him on a camel in Egypt. There are souvenir handkerchiefs Cecil bought in Cairo for his brothers, and a silk, embroidered postcard and cushion cover for Elizabeth, all still in beautiful condition.

At the heart of the display are artefacts associated with Cecil's death, beginning with the telegram announcing that he had been killed. This was sent to the local Anglican minister in Uralla, Reverend E.H. Stammer, so he could break the news to Elizabeth. Very few of these telegrams have survived, but obviously Reverend Stammer left this one with her and she kept it. Cecil's campaign medals are there, along with a photograph of his grave at the Brewery Orchard Cemetery at Bois-Grenier, near Armentières, in France. Elizabeth's last letters to Cecil were returned to her stamped "deceased" because he'd died before he could receive them.

Then there are the personal effects sent by military authorities to Elizabeth after Cecil's death. Every deceased soldier's service file records the effects, if any, returned to the family and, as on Cecil's file, they are always listed with brutal simplicity: photo, metal brooch, knife, letter, papers, disc, belt, badge, notebooks, "devotional" books, and so on. I have often brooded over these lists, but I have never seen the actual things laid out like this, almost complete. They were usually disbursed among the family as keepsakes, but here Elizabeth kept nearly all of them herself.

I stood looking at Cecil Stoker's last possessions. New Testament, prayer book and notebook. A belt covered in a schoolboy-ish collection of buttons and badges. A tin of curios. Two saucy postcards he'd obviously picked up while on leave somewhere, never thinking his mother would see them. A photograph of a young girl in a white dress and wide-brimmed white hat (not Vida, as it turned out, but a girl called Amy). The knife and identity disc are not there, so perhaps Cecil's brothers managed to grab a souvenir each.

Elizabeth kept all Cecil's letters, and her letters to him have also survived. Museum volunteers have faithfully transcribed them for visitors to read. It is quite unusual to have the complete exchange; generally, a soldier's letters from the front are the ones offered to archives and libraries, while the family's letters to him either don't survive or aren't considered historically important enough for posterity.

Elizabeth wrote to "Ces" every week and was always anxious for letters from him. She chats about local comings and goings, although Uralla is very quiet with so many men away. Mrs Besley is knitting Ces some socks. A man from Newcastle named Solomon wants to buy her business and she is considering it (ultimately, she doesn't sell). She will be closing the shop for a few hours on 25 April 1916 "in commemoration of Anzac Day". It is also six years since "poor dad died" and she is feeling very miserable. She sends Ces parcel after parcel: socks, biscuits, tins of cheese, sheep's tongues and salmon, preserved fruit, lollies, soap, coffee, milk. What else could she do? "I hope you will enjoy them," she writes.

* * *

At the funeral address for Elizabeth Stoker, the local minister declared she had been a loving and devoted mother, a faithful daughter within the church who had earned the esteem of a wide circle of friends. No doubt she had. By then the double-boxed family archive had already been hidden away for three years, and to me it feels like Elizabeth had long sealed off her deepest feelings about Cecil's loss. The boxing could have been her act of emotional independence, a declaration that she had never wanted anyone's sympathy, and when she began preparing for her own death she hated the thought of anyone, even her family, going through her things and feeling sorry for her all over again.

What if, instead of passively weeping and writing nice little thank you notes to people who sent condolences after Ces died, Elizabeth Stoker took herself out on winter nights through the frosty paddocks around Uralla where no-one could hear her, lifted her head, and screamed and howled at a non-existent god for taking her husband and son? By herself, with only a few startled sheep to witness a rage so vast it couldn't be absorbed by conventional gestures and memorials – only by an open sky and distant, icy stars.

Arthur Stace's Single Mighty Word

In my part of the world, fewer and fewer people seem to remember Arthur Stace. Younger friends and colleagues will frown awkwardly at the mention of someone they think they should know about, but really don't. "The Eternity man," I prompt. That bloke who wrote the word "Eternity" in chalk thousands of times on footpaths in Sydney. Remember when "Eternity" was illuminated on the Sydney Harbour Bridge on 1 January 2000?

Perhaps it's understandable: this is a Sydney story, and I live in Canberra. In Sydney his memory seems to be still strong – although, since Stace died in 1967, fewer people will remember having discovered an "Eternity" inscribed by the man himself in his famous elaborate copperplate. It would be even rarer to find someone who actually glimpsed him at work in the pre-dawn, head bowed, kneeling to leave his one-word message in chalk or crayon.

I became curious about Stace during trips to Sydney in the 1990s, when a highlight was to call in at the Remo store in Darlinghurst to browse all manner of cool stuff you probably didn't need but was fun to own, including t-shirts, prints and other merch emblazoned with Stace's "Eternity" in a design by Martin Sharp. The artist had been incorporating Stace's "Eternity" into his work for years, and a five-metre rendition on canvas adorned Remo's Crown Street window – stopping traffic, according to proprietor Remo Giuffré. From

Arthur Stace, 1963
Photographer: Trevor Dallen
Sydney Morning Herald

beyond the grave, Stace was very good to Remo. "We were never ones to miss a good merchandising opportunity," he recalled.

Stace's fame peaked in the 1990s, but Sydney had always been fascinated by him. From the 1930s onwards the discovery of an "Eternity" on a pavement or wall was a unique and unifying experience for Sydney residents. Graffiti was still uncommon, and the letters were so perfectly formed, the meaning so tantalising. Who was this Eternity man? No-one knew. By the 1950s there were so many rumours, so much press speculation, and increasing numbers of false claims by impostors, that in 1956 Stace allowed his identity to be revealed. By 1965 he estimated he had written "Eternity" 500,000 times all over Sydney.

* * *

Stace's story, as he told it, was that he was born into poverty. His parents, two brothers and two sisters (actually, he had three sisters) were all alcoholics, he said, and he himself was a drifter, a petty criminal and an alcoholic for decades before he converted to Christianity. That happened after he joined, by chance, a service in August 1930 at St Barnabas's Anglican Church, Broadway, on the promise of tea and cake afterwards. The preacher was the Reverend R.B.S. Hammond, famous in Sydney as a "mender of broken men" – men like Arthur Stace who believed themselves beyond help. Years later Stace was fond of saying that he went in for rock cake and came out with "the Rock of Ages". He gave up alcohol and was befriended by Hammond, who gave him a job at the Hammond Hotel, a hostel he ran in Chippendale. Stace worked in its emergency depot helping men in need of a wash and a shave, or repairs to their clothes and boots.

Spiritually, though, Stace was more drawn to the services at the Burton Street Tabernacle, a Baptist church in Darlinghurst. There, in 1932, he heard a sermon by a famous evangelical preacher of the day, John Ridley. "Eternity! Eternity!" Ridley cried. "I wish I could sound, or shout, that word to everyone in the streets of Sydney. Eternity! You have got to meet it. Where will you spend eternity?" Stace was profoundly moved. Leaving the church, he discovered a piece of chalk in his pocket and bent down and wrote "Eternity" there and then on the ground. He joined the community at Burton Street, and that was the beginning of his new life as a reformed alcoholic and self-described "missioner" seeking to convert others.

When an energetic new pastor, Lisle Thompson, arrived at Burton Street in 1951 the two men immediately became friends. One day, after an outdoor service, Thompson spotted Stace at work with his chalk: "So you're Mr Eternity, Arthur," he queried. "Guilty, your honour" was the reply. Thompson wanted to share Stace's story and eventually he persuaded Stace that an account of his conversion, written as a "tract", would be a good evangelistic tool, an exemplar for others. Titled *The Crooked Made Straight*, Thompson's eight-page account briefly noted that Stace was the Eternity man. "This one-word sermon has challenged thousands and thousands," he added.

However, seeing the tract circulating quietly among churches was not enough for Thompson, and finally Stace let him take "Mr Eternity" to the press. The scoop went to Tom Farrell at the *Daily Telegraph* and the story covered six columns in the Sunday edition on 24 June 1956. The mystery was solved, and overnight Arthur Stace, living modestly in Pyrmont with his wife, Pearl (they met through church activities and married in 1942), became one of Sydney's most famous citizens.

* * *

In the ensuing years Stace was happy to grant a further press interview now and then. In 1965, two years before his death, he told a journalist that he had tried a few different slogans – "Obey God", for instance – but that "I think eternity gets the message across, makes people stop and think." It certainly did, but what Stace might not have realised was that with increasing material prosperity, secularism and multiculturalism in Australia, younger people were becoming baffled.

Martin Sharp first spotted an "Eternity" in 1953 when he was just eleven, and he was captivated. "What does it mean? Why is it there? Who wrote it?" He didn't learn the full story of Arthur Stace until 1983 when he was given a copy of Keith Dunstan's book *Ratbags*, published in 1979. Arthur Stace was one of Dunstan's "ratbags" along with Percy Grainger, Barry Humphries, Frank Thring and others of that ilk. Meanwhile, in 1958 journalist Gavin Souter had compared Stace to bohemian rebel Bea Miles and other Sydney "characters", including a man who sat perfectly still on a bench in Hyde Park with an open packet of peanuts in his lap, covered head to foot in pigeons. In 2001 Peter Carey declared that Sydney didn't love Stace because he was "saved" but because he was "a drunk, a ratbag, an outcast ... a slave to no one on this earth". Clive James in 2003 simply called him a "lonely madman".

Christians, on the other hand, had little difficulty in interpreting Stace's message the way he meant it – that there is a life after this one and we need to be prepared for it. For them there was nothing peculiar about a devout Christian wanting to spread such a message. In 1994 the Reverend Bernard Judd, an Anglican rector and long-time friend of Stace, declared emphatically in a filmed interview that Arthur was not a fanatic, not obsessed, and rejected the association with Sydney's eccentrics. Stace was "a thoroughgoing reasonable rational Christian".

When a full biography of Stace, *Mr Eternity: The story of Arthur Stace*, appeared in 2017 it was published by the Bible Society. The avowedly Christian co-authors, Roy Williams and Elizabeth Meyers (the latter a daughter of Stace's friend Lisle Thompson), reiterated Judd's assessment to again counter the idea that Stace was a "weirdo", or mentally ill. He was unusual, they conceded, but that could be said of any "prodigious achiever" in human history.

Poet Douglas Stewart could embrace the sublime and transcendent in Stace while avoiding the preachy context, and in so doing helped propel Stace's work into our modern, secular age. The oft-quoted first stanza of his poem "Arthur Stace", first published in 1969, runs thus:

> That shy mysterious poet Arthur Stace
> Whose work was just one single mighty word
> Walked in the utmost depths of time and space
> And there his word was spoken and he heard
> *Eternity, Eternity*, it banged him like a bell
> Dulcet from heaven sounding, sombre from hell.

Stewart's poem helped inspire Lawrence Johnston's documentary *Eternity* in 1994. Parts of the poem are read during the film, and its beautiful cinematography encompassed a similar sense of light, shadow and mystery. The soundtrack was adapted from Ross Edwards's haunting orchestral work *Symphony Da Pacem Domine*. Like Stewart, Johnston wanted to explore Stace's part in the biography of Sydney, and black-and-white re-creations feature an actor (Les Foxcroft) as a silent, lonely, Stace-like figure in an overcoat and hat, head bowed, walking, kneeling and chalking. An assembly of people, including Bernard Judd, Martin Sharp and artist George Gittoes, describe how Stace had motivated them and stirred their imaginations.

Gittoes was one of the few to have witnessed Stace at work. He recalled staring idly into a shop window early one morning in 1964 when he became aware of the image of a man reflected from across the street. As he watched, silently, unwilling to interrupt, the man knelt "almost as if in prayer" and wrote something on the ground. Gittoes had never heard of Arthur Stace then and thought that "Eternity" had been written just for him. As a fifteen-year-old boy "looking for signs", he said, that one word seemed to be "like a whole book of words", and the experience had remained "like a tattoo on [his] soul" ever since. There was something else that struck the artist's eye, and he remembered it even after thirty years: Stace's shoes were too big. As the man knelt, Gittoes could see clearly into the gap between his sock and his shoe.

I too am fascinated by this detail. Everyone remembers Stace as a carefully dressed man, always in a suit, tie and felt hat, and an overcoat for winter. The few photographs of him attest to this. But Gittoes noticed that his shoes were much too big, clearly not originally his own. This could have been because as a small man, only five foot three, Stace had trouble finding shoes that fit. Or because even in the relative comfort of his later years Stace was still too frugal to buy new shoes. Whatever the case, my imagination gets to work in that gap between the actual man and how he presented himself to the world.

Stace's adeptness at controlling his own story for public consumption leads me to wonder: what was in the gap? What was he not telling us? What would drive someone to write "Eternity" on the footpath every day for thirty-seven years? Half a million times. Was Stace "unusual"? Obviously. A "madman"? Unhelpful. "Obsessed"? Yes, I think so.

* * *

Arthur Stace as depot manager at the Hammond Hotel in the 1930s
HammondCare Archives

Stace was always a poor man, but the dimensions and impact of that poverty have until recently been under-appreciated. The trauma that would afflict his life began even before he was born. His biographers have shown that his mother, Laura Lewis, had two children with an unknown father, or fathers, while she was a teenager living at home with her parents in Windsor, New South Wales. The first baby died, and the second, Clara, born in 1876, nearly did too.

What happened was this. One day Laura left the three-month-old with her own mother, Margaret Lewis, while she visited a neighbour. Ten minutes later Laura was called home to find Clara pitifully unwell. Margaret claimed to have given her granddaughter a drink of tea, but a doctor was called and, as he later testified, found the baby suffering from "gastric irritation of the stomach and bowels", retching and crying incessantly. Soon it was discovered that what Margaret had actually given Clara was carbolic acid, a common disinfectant. A local chemist testified that he had sold it, diluted in oil, to Laura during her pregnancy to treat an abscess.

Remarkably, Clara survived, and although Margaret appeared before a magistrate, a murder charge seems to have been dropped. Why? If Margaret had been making a sudden wild attempt to eliminate an unwanted mouth to feed, there seems to have been insufficient evidence for a conviction. Stace's biographers, Williams and Meyers, offer the simple conclusion that it was a genuine accident in a chaotic household.

Four years later, in 1880, Margaret's husband John was imprisoned for assaulting her, and on his release in 1882 immediately sought her out and assaulted her again. Evidence suggests that the whole family lived in fear of this man. Laura escaped to Sydney with Clara but found no real refuge there. She took up with William Stace, an Englishman from a modestly prosperous background, and together they had six children; Arthur was the second youngest, born in 1885.

But William was feckless and, in the deepening depression of the 1890s, could not hold down a job. The family moved frequently among Sydney's cramped inner-city suburbs, sliding into poverty. By

1892 they were accepting charity, and in November William Stace deserted the family, leaving Laura destitute. Her only option was the Benevolent Society Asylum, a huge institution located near where Central Station is today. After a Christmas spent within those grim walls, Arthur, his older brother William and younger brother Samuel were fostered. Arthur was seven.

Williams and Meyers mention that later in life Arthur would not speak of his time in foster care. The years he blanked out were spent with a family in Goulburn. Later he was placed with families in Wollongong, and as a teenager he found employment in the coalmines there. (With his first pay, he said, he bought a drink: the first step towards decades of alcohol addiction.) The Stace family was scattered. William and Laura reconciled, but their lives were marred by alcohol and violence, and all their children were fostered or left of their own accord. By the time Arthur returned to Sydney in about 1905, when he was twenty, William had become a chronic and violent alcoholic, and Laura appears to have taken to prostitution. William died in the Parramatta Hospital for the Insane in November 1908, aged about fifty-two. Laura died of cancer in 1912.

Considering all this, the gaps and inconsistencies in Stace's account of his life are unsurprising. I think he exaggerated his and his family's criminal associations a little, probably to make his conversion in 1930 seem more powerful. Especially interesting is his claim that as a child he had very little schooling, and that he couldn't account for his ability to write "Eternity", and only that word, in perfect copperplate. He implied it was done by some kind of divine guidance, but there is ample evidence that he could write quite well and had obviously received some primary education. When Stace said he couldn't write, the deprivation he was describing was perhaps not education – it was love.

* * *

The gap between the shoe and the sock turns out to be vast. It's not just the gap between Stace the man and what he said about himself, but the gap between the historical sources (newly digitised, many of them) and how we interpret those sources in our own times. I suggest that what was in that gap was intergenerational poverty, violence, substance abuse and trauma. The twin pillars of Stace's trauma may have been, first, the poisoning of his half-sister Clara in 1876, and later, his separation from his parents and siblings when he was seven.

What *happened* on that day in Windsor in 1876? There was baby Clara, "retching and crying". There was the shock, the panic, the tears and outrage, and the smell of carbolic around Clara's mouth. All the witnesses would have had their versions of events, but only the baby's grandmother really knew, and how could Margaret have explained her actions if she herself was a victim of earlier circumstances impossible to describe? How did Laura cope with the memory of that day, and how could she establish a future for herself and her children? Whom could she trust? Not William Stace, as it turned out.

Arthur's early childhood memories were of sleeping on bags under the house when his parents were "on the drink", and having to steal milk from verandas and food from bakers' carts and shops. Fostering might have given him and his brothers proper beds, food and clothing, but at the cost of everything and everyone they had ever known. Did they know about the events in Windsor? From under the house, they might have picked up bits of it from abusive arguments between their parents. Or perhaps it was never mentioned. Either way, spoken of or not, the story was surely always *there*, impossible to un-remember.

Our increasing knowledge of trauma and its effects on mind and body may offer new insights into Stace's behaviour as an adult. For years, both before and after his identity as "Mr Eternity" became known, he told his story many times in church services and prayer meetings: how he had been brought up in a "vile" environment, how he had lived a "slothful drunken life", going from job to job, jail to jail, and how finally, at his lowest point, he had been "plucked from the fires of hell" at St Barnabas's when "the spirit of the living God" entered his life. It was (and is) common in Baptist services for people to give "testimony" in this way by describing their lives before and after conversion. Here then was an accepted language and a template for Stace to craft a narrative of his own.

Conversion gave Stace not just a community to belong to – probably for the first time ever – but an accepting audience. He could stand outside his story and gain comforting distance from it, always with a group of the faithful to take it and hold it for him without judgement.

So then, those half-million eternities could have been another form of repetitious behaviour, born of trauma. His message could have been not only a one-word sermon or a one-word poem, but a one-word trauma narrative. Mightily told, over and over. In those daily pre-dawn excursions around Sydney, the act of kneeling to write "Eternity" every few hundred yards might have put Stace into a meditative state, separated from his past, eternally in the present. Hoping, with his chalk-dry fingers, to convert his suffering into something redemptive for other people.

Afternoon Tea with Mary Gilmore

If I could have visited Mary Gilmore at her home in King's Cross, Sydney, I wonder what she would have made of me? This meeting could never have occurred – Gilmore died in 1962, aged ninety-seven – but still I imagine myself mounting the stairs to her first-floor flat at 99 Darlinghurst Road, where she had lived since 1933, and nervously knocking on her door.

The great writer has spent the morning making jam, and the flat is still heavy with the scent. A little jar is set aside for me to take home. Dame Mary likes making jam, but as she escorts me in she's quick to notice that any talk about the ratio of fruit to sugar is wasted on me. I've never had time to make jam.

My hostess sets about making yerba maté tea for me, chatting about how she acquired a taste for it during her years in South America. She had travelled to Paraguay in 1896 to join the utopian socialist settlement known as Cosme, where she met and married her Australian husband, Will Gilmore. After the failure of the settlement in 1900 they had moved to Argentina with their baby son, Billy, while Will worked to pay for their passage home.

Forty years later the Australian magazine *Pix* published a feature on Mary Gilmore, who was famous by then as a journalist, poet and social reformer, and photographed her at home drinking yerba maté the traditional way from a gourd, using a straw known as a *bombilla*. Today, though, she presents it to me from a teapot. I was expecting a bitter, grassy concoction but it was actually quite mild and pleasant. The critical thing, Dame Mary tells me as we settle down in her cluttered living room, is to brew it gently in water that is *hot* but not *boiling*.

When journalist Leslie Rees visited Mary Gilmore at home in 1936, his impression of her was of "living eyes, richly, deeply brown as the eyes of William Butler Yeats, in a face that shows the scars of a life faced with dignity and intelligence". Her brain was "as active and unsentimental as an electrical coil". Bright and lively conversation was said to be the essence of life to Mary Gilmore, and that's partly why I'm nervous; I'm not a sparkling conversationalist myself. So it's a relief when the heavily underlined copies of *Soviet Weekly* are set aside and she waits with a kindly look for me to broach the subject I'd come to talk about.

I ask her about the years she spent editing the women's page of the Australian Workers' Union paper, the *Worker*. I tell her I'm especially interested in the first pages she edited, published in January 1908. She had called on women to write to her on any subject that interested them, and to share their knowledge, even just little labour-saving procedures in the kitchen, with other readers. Her hope was to get at the "needs, the hopes and fears and desires" of all women, in a "bond of unity" from one end of the country to another.

Ah yes, she muses. She had wondered how to educate women about how politics and current events could affect their lives. But how do you reach the tired woman rocking the baby's cradle with her foot while she peels potatoes or darns stockings in her lap? Such a woman, Dame Mary chuckles, has no time to read the prime minister's thoughts on tariff reform.

"So, women did write to you?"

"Oh, my word, yes! About all sorts of things, very personal sometimes. Distressing. And the questions I got! From men as well. People seemed to think I was a one-woman encyclopedia. Has the price of calico gone down? How do you make soap? How do you get rid of fleas? Once I even published a poem about my weekly mailbag."

"Yes, I've read that."

"Have you indeed!" She pauses. "So why are you here?"

"Do you still have the letters women wrote to you?"

Dame Mary stares.

"No. Why should I? I dealt with them and threw them in the wastepaper basket."

I picture all that history consigned to an overflowing wastepaper basket.

"Look around you. I don't have space to keep that kind of thing. Do you know how many times I had to move house in those years?"

"No."

"Actually, nor do I any more. But it was a lot."

"I wanted to see the originals of the letters."

"Why? They weren't written to you."

She leans forward.

"What exactly you are searching for?"

* * *

What indeed? What was it that brought me in my imagination as a suppliant to Mary Gilmore's door?

Mary Gilmore, c. 1952
State Library of Victoria 9917795523607636

I had become interested in Gilmore's editorship of the *Worker* women's page because out of it emerged one of Australia's most successful community cookbooks. The recipes and household hints section had been so popular that she compiled the contributions into a book, *The Worker Cook Book*, published by the paper in 1914. It went through ten editions between then and 1919.

A trail through secondary sources led me to Gilmore's papers at the National Library of Australia in Canberra, where apparently there were letters from women who had written to her in response to the cookbook. They survived because the frugally minded poet had used the backs of them as scrap paper to draft her poems.

With archives you may get something or you may get nothing at all, I'm well aware of that, but still I dreamed of a feast of untapped primary source material. The cookbook would provide the necessary narrative focus for a kitchen-window glimpse into the domestic lives of working-class women more than a hundred years ago. The archival material would be exactly as I imagined it would be, and the result would be awesome.

Not. The trail turned out to be false, at least as far as the cookbook was concerned. There *are* letters from readers within files of Gilmore's drafts of published and unpublished poems. I found about eighty, in MS 727 series one, two, three and nine; and in MS 8766 box two. Unfortunately, they can't be identified from the library's finding aids because the archivist who described the records didn't think them important enough to note.

Only a handful of the letters refer to the cookbook, and then just in passing. The handwritten drafts of poems were often illegible (although, as Gilmore might say, they weren't written for me) and the reverses were usually blank. My project on *The Worker Cook Book* collapsed before my eyes. I wasn't going to give up; I'd stay for whatever I could find. I must have turned over thousands of handwritten and typed sheets. On and on, turning, turning, rocking myself mentally to sleep in the peaceful hush of the library reading room.

Suddenly, this: "... a worm will turn. When we think of all the suffering that is all over the world and for what purpose, it seems for one class only and it is time the working class woke up and got their rights." I was wide awake now too. Who was this? Mrs E. Birch, whoever she was. I only had the second page of her letter, no address and no date. She has been reading the *Worker* for two years, she says, and finds it appeals to her "way of thinking". She and her husband were on an "estate" as a married couple, but to live and save from a man's weekly wage was "impossible".

More turning. Maud Woodbury from Cessnock wrote in 1918 to ask Gilmore to send a word of friendship and cheer to some "lonely sister" of the "never-never country". She enclosed a second letter for Gilmore to forward to anyone she knew who might appreciate it. "Those brave, quiet women of the glorious proletariat always fill me with deepest admiration and sympathy."

A mother wrote a frantic account of her baby's illness, but I only had the second page of her letter. A doctor had advised her to stop breastfeeding and give the baby whey, but she refused. "I gave her castor oil and looked to my own health." The baby was weaned eventually onto Glaxo (a baby formula) but "one tin nearly killed her". She tried barley water and Nestlé's Milk Food. The baby developed a fever and gastritis. There was a hospital visit. Nearly at the bottom of the page now. Barley water again, and white of egg, and brandy. "I gave her ..." – and there it ends.

A mother of six wrote in 1920 from Woolbrook, south of Armidale, to ask how to find a book on midwifery because she was anxious to help pregnant women in her town with their births, there being no doctor or nurse for sixteen miles. She had written to the state government and been told that such a book would not be suitable for "inexperienced women". May Kent from East Moree wrote in 1920 about an elderly woman living alone next door who, because of a horror of being buried a "pauper", had "done without many a little thing to put a couple of shillings away". This woman had been told that if it was discovered that she had money in the bank it would interfere with her pension. Could Mrs Gilmore advise on this point?

I found many of those much smaller questions that obviously caused Gilmore so much amused exasperation. J.M. Mann from Wyalong wanted information on how to rear young parrots – blue bonnets and "bullan bullans" (ringnecks) – because oatmeal had failed and his birds had died. Jessie English from South Gippsland asked if the Australian School of Sketching in Sydney was a genuine establishment or a "swindle". George Ritter from Narrabri had "scurf" in his hair and sickness in his fowls.

Then there were the letters from children. Every week Gilmore published a selection of these and, perhaps recalling her own childhood, tended to favour those from children in remote places. Joyce Jones from Pine Ridge in northern New South Wales wrote in 1918: "I am nearly twelve years old and would like some girls to write to me we have three cats and three cows and I am very fond of reading my Uncle takes the worker we live almost on the bank of the Marra Creek." I was charmed to discover letters from two sisters, written on successive days in October 1917, asking to be put in touch with pen-friends. Lilly and Annie Hasted wrote from Listowel Downs via Blackall, south of Barcaldine in Queensland. Both remarked on their faraway home. "It is very lonely out here," wrote Annie, aged twelve.

Sometimes all I found was a torn fragment. "Well Mrs Gilmore," wrote someone from Burrandong via Mumbil in 1919, "after reading those pitiful letters in the Worker about tired Mothers I think it is something terrible my mother is only a poor woman and we have to battle through the world as good as we can there are ..." – and the rest of the sheet is torn off. Most perplexing of all was a sheet torn vertically rather than horizontally, leaving only the right-hand side of the page. The letter was from a child, apparently a regular correspondent, along with her sister, to the *Worker*. Since her last letter there had been a flood at their place, she says, and she is knitting a sock. Here I did study what Gilmore had written on the other side, a lullaby. I wondered if the narrow width of the sheet had helped Gilmore to keep the lines short as she drafted the poem. Here are the first two verses.

> Here we go
> Sleepy slow
> Rockabye baby
> Bye O
>
> Still little foot
> Still little hand
> Hushabye baby
> Bye O

Gilmore's women's page was much more than an advice column. Each page typically carried several leading articles written by Gilmore herself in which she explored her many cherished causes. These could include the need to introduce an aged pension; the plight of rural women living in poverty; poor treatment of female servants and prisoners; the introduction of maternity allowances, child endowment and pre- and post-natal care for mothers; and women's rights to living wages and equal opportunities, and indeed the same rights as men to freedom, independence and happiness.

Readers' letters were nevertheless vital in informing Gilmore's advocacy on these and other issues. In her twenty-three years editing the page, Gilmore must have read thousands of letters from readers, especially women. Some were published in full, others were summarised into copy that Gilmore would write, often with added commentary of her own.

Today the *Worker* (known from 1913 onwards as the *Australian Worker*) is fully digitised and available via the National Library's Trove website, making this vast corpus of Gilmore's work is now fully searchable. I could therefore discover if the readers' letters I saw in Gilmore's personal papers were published or mentioned, but of the selection noted above I could only trace the letters from Joyce Jones, the Hasted sisters and the man rearing parrots. Of the rest, nothing. So I can't say whether the sick baby survived or the woman from Woolbrook received her midwifery book or the caring woman received advice for her pensioner neighbour.

But the correspondent who mentioned tired mothers was responding to a regular theme on the *Worker*'s page. In 1914 Gilmore published some poems (not her own) titled "Tired Mothers", which initiated a stream of letters well into the 1920s. Women wrote that they were exhausted with childrearing and housework and the strain of feeding their children on their husbands' low wages. Of how sad it made them that their children could rarely eat fruit and vegetables except potatoes or receive a new toy at Christmas. That they would rather die themselves than bring any more children into the world.

Gilmore was proud to have published as many of these letters as she could because, she claimed, no women's column in any other paper

Mary Gilmore, 1916
Photographer: May Moore
State Library of New South Wales 9AL4k6kY

was bothering. "They come to me by every mail. The saddest things can never be published; they are too individual and too private – and sometimes too terrible." The suffering of other people never failed to move and inspire Mary Gilmore to action, because she had known loneliness herself. Life as a bush wife on the Gilmore family farm in Victoria had been unbearable for her, and in 1911 she and Will decided to live apart. Their adored son Billy went with Mary to Sydney, but as soon as he was old enough he joined his father working properties in

Queensland. Mary and Will still regarded themselves as a couple, but the family was seldom together.

So although she relished her independent existence in Sydney as a celebrated poet and journalist, Gilmore missed the intimacy of a small family circle and she was constantly torn between love, duty, work and family. Her own warm and compassionate manner was very evident to readers.

Relations between Gilmore and the management of the *Worker* deteriorated throughout the 1920s, and in February 1931 she resigned. In a long, angry letter to the president of the Australian Workers' Union, John Barnes, she declared that in addition to her published work for the paper, there had been considerable extra labour – unpaid and unthanked – privately answering letters from thousands of "poor souls" who had had no-one else to turn to. Drunken husbands, persecuting policemen, unwanted babies, family maintenance, workers' compensation, pensions: she dealt with them all. "From New Zealand to Tasmania, from Sydney to Port Darwin, you will find letters of mine in every direction." And they had not cost the union even the postage stamp that carried them.

A diagonal line across each of the readers' letters I saw in her papers suggests that Gilmore had dealt with them, if not by publication then by private reply. This gets me imagining the arrival into thousands of homes of a letter from that much-loved author Mary Gilmore. Many a woman must have quietly slipped one into her apron pocket to study later, anxiously, by the fire, when the family was asleep. I don't consider Gilmore an "agony aunt" in the modern sense because, in print at least, she mainly focused on responses to practical problems. In those less explicit times, her readers' emotional and sexual difficulties were probably among the things she believed "too terrible" to publish.

They are gone, most of them, those readers' letters to Mary Gilmore, and her private replies are also scattered and lost. Yes, her journalism for the *Worker* does incorporate many of them in one form or another, and yes, digitisation opens up research pathways undreamed of in an analogue age. So then, why chase what is not there to be found? Sometimes I think of a line from Tennyson's "Ulysses" (one of my father's favourite poems): "Tho' much is taken, much abides."

But in archives the reverse can apply: much abides but much has been taken. That loss is not *nothing*; it leaves a trace. The letters and letter fragments I found at the National Library pointed so powerfully to what was *not* there that for a while all I could do was sit there, rigid with disappointment. Still, within that absence there was also an encounter with aspects of myself: my desire to gather up what is lost, mend what is broken, and bear witness to the uniqueness of every human experience.

* * *

"There is something I *can* show you, though."

"Oh yes?"

"On the table over there, that little card. Bring it here."

She turns it over in her old fingers. On the front is an illustration of a kitten with a blue bow around its neck, holding a bunch of flowers.

"I was on television, you know."

"Yes, I saw it. I can't believe they brought all their cameras and things in here."

"So tiring." But she is smiling.

She hands me the card. It's from a ten-year-old girl, Christine Higgs of East Maitland. Christine had carefully dated it 12 June 1959. She wrote to say that she had seen the telecast from Dame Mary's flat.

"I enjoyed it. I heard your poems, and I also saw your kettle boiling."

On the back of the card she had written out a poem of Dame Mary's she had learned at school.

"Read it for me."

The Fairy Man

It was, it was a fairy man
Who came to town today.
"I'll make a cake for sixpence,
If you will pay, will pay."

He iced it with a moonbeam
And found a penny, too;
He made a cake of rainbows,
And baked it in the dew.

"I read that one at school too. But I think Christine has muddled the lines a bit..."

I look up. Dame Mary is asleep.

Lifting the Shadow

Queer history in Australia received a considerable fillip in 2023 with the broadcast of the three-part series *Queerstralia* by the ABC. Timed to coincide with WorldPride in Sydney in February–March, its upbeat and affirming style treated the troubled aspects of queer history with a relatively light touch. It demonstrated that the energy in queer history tends to form around legal reform and the advancement of LGBTQIA+ rights from the 1970s onwards.

To research and write queer history before living memory – without oral testimony, that is – is to enter a much darker place. The last man to hang for sodomy in the British Empire was in Tasmania in 1867, and in 1997 Tasmania became the last Australian jurisdiction to decriminalise male homosexuality. Relationships and life choices that are criminalised, stigmatised and pathologised are unlikely to leave much of an imprint on the public record, and surviving historical evidence is often patchy, obscure and cloaked in euphemism.

In 1990 I wrote an honours thesis in the history department of the University of Tasmania on the Tasmanian writer Roy Bridges. Most of Bridges's thirty-six novels were adventure stories for boys or middle-brow historical romances and melodramas dealing with the early days of Tasmania and Victoria. Frequently he was inspired by stories his mother, Laura Wood, told of her family history on their farm near Sorell, east of Hobart, going back to the beginning of white settlement. Bridges was Tasmania's most prolific novelist, successful and admired

Roy Bridges, 1937
State Library of Victoria 9934763393607636

in his time, but his reputation didn't outlast his death in 1952. I wasn't interested in the quality of his writing so much as his interpretation of Tasmanian colonial history, and how his own deep connection with the island was refracted through his works of fiction and memoir.

Born in Hobart in 1885, Bridges started to be published in 1909, and at first wrote for the gutsy little New South Wales Bookstall Company. Time and again he sold his copyright for fifty pounds per novel, whenever he was hard up ("which was often"), grateful for the support the Bookstall gave to new Australian writers. In his mature period his novels were published in London by Hutchinson or Hodder & Stoughton, but during and after the Second World War his output declined. The gratifying success of *That Yesterday Was Home* (1948) eased his final years. Part history, part family history and part memoir, this is an uneven but passionately expressed meditation on memory and connection with place.

By the time I started work on Bridges he was remembered mainly by enthusiasts interested in the literary culture of Tasmania. As a thesis project he was perfect. No-one else was claiming him, and significant collections of his papers were held in libraries in Hobart, Melbourne and Canberra. Methodologically I had Bridges's memoir as a guide, which, unreliable as any memoir always is – and I knew this – was at least a place to begin. I bought a 1:25,000 map of the Sorell district and pinned it to my wall in the history department. I drove out to meet Bridges's nephew and his family, who were still working the property that Bridges had named "Woods" after his mother's family.

The town of Sorell has always been a stopping point for travellers from Hobart heading either to the east coast or to the convict ruins at Port Arthur. To get there you must first drive across Frederick Henry Bay via the Sorell causeway at Pitt Water. "All my life," Bridges wrote in 1948, "Frederick Henry Bay has sounded through my mind and imagination. Like drums ... or like cannonade in storm, or in the frozen stillness of winter's nights." Every time I drive across the Sorell causeway I think of him, and did so again one brilliant day in February 2023 while heading up to Bicheno on holiday. With the sun sparkling off the bay I shouldn't have been brooding on old stories, but suddenly I knew that the time was right to tackle again a biographical dilemma I had evaded, all those years ago.

The few others who have written about Bridges have struggled to understand the source of the loneliness and sorrow which, towards the end, amounted to torment. His journalist friend C.E. (Ted) Sayers first met Bridges in 1922 and remembered him as a haunted, "tense little man", a chain-smoker, embarrassed in the company of women, who had allowed a streak of morbidity and violence to enter his fiction. I developed my own suspicions about this haunting, and in my thesis in 1990 I speculated, briefly and carefully (because this was

Tasmania), that Roy Bridges had been a closeted and deeply repressed gay man.

I wouldn't have thought of this except for a conversation I had with the one friend of Bridges I could still find, a well-known local historian named Basil Rait. I visited the elderly Mr Rait in a tumbledown house in north Hobart somewhere near Trinity Church. Just as I was deciding that his recollections weren't going to be particularly useful, he astounded me with the remark that one day, Roy Bridges had been seen emerging from the Imperial Hotel on Collins Street in central Hobart, and that the Imperial was a known place for homosexual men to congregate.

When did this occur? And did Rait see this himself? I was too amazed – and too timid, I think – to ask enough questions and, rookie historian that I was, I did not record the conversation. Why was Rait so frank, and what did he think I would do with his information? Perhaps I'd gained his trust *because* I had arrived without a tape recorder. I don't know. But I did consider his revelation very carefully. The once-elegant Imperial was rather seedy by then, which seemed to lend plausibility to what Rait had said. I had gay friends and I asked if anyone knew anything about the Imperial's reputation. No-one did.

Unable to verify Rait's assertion, I turned to the textual sources. Although I was aware of the danger of reading too much into odd snippets of evidence that might have signified nothing, I was also unwilling to ignore what I had been told, which, if true, might explain everything. To speculate about Bridges's sexuality in the thesis, or not: my thesis supervisor left it up to me. On an early draft I can see in his handwriting: "You decide."

* * *

Royal Tasman (Roy) Bridges came from a family of prosperous wicker manufacturers and retailers. His father, Samuel, and uncle James ran Bridges Brothers, in Elizabeth Street, Hobart, which had been founded in 1857 by their father, Samuel senior. After graduating with an arts degree from the University of Tasmania, Bridges joined the *Tasmanian News* as a cadet in December 1904. Journalism was his career for most of the next twenty-five years. He accepted a job with the Hobart *Mercury* in 1907 but soon became disaffected by poorly paid sixteen-hour days on what his memoir described as a "rotten sweatrag", and so he headed for Sydney.

He got a job immediately on the *Australian Star* under its editor, Ralph Asher. Sydney was a relief from Hobart's "superficial puritanism, social restrictions and moral repressions of human nature", but in 1909 the chance of a job on the *Age* lured him to Melbourne, where he settled in happily for a decade. Then, between 1919 and 1935 (after which he retired permanently to the farm back in Sorell) he mixed freelance writing with journalism, mostly with the *Age* but also, briefly and unhappily, with the Melbourne *Herald* in 1927.

A shy man, Bridges did love the companionship of other journalists. Keith Murdoch, future father of Rupert, was one of his early friends on the *Age*, although they didn't remain close. There was Neville Ussher, of the *Argus* and the *Age*, who died during the First World War and whose photograph Bridges kept close to him for the rest of his life. And then there was Phillip Schuler, son of Frederick Schuler, editor of the *Age*.

High-spirited, charming, handsome: Phillip Schuler's nickname was "Peter" because of his Peter Pan personality. Friendship "blossomed" during a bushwalk on a "golden August Sunday at Oakleigh" – then only sparsely settled – and after that the two young men spent many weekends together. They read the same books, roistered in restaurants and theatres, and tried their hands at writing plays.

On a walking holiday in Tasmania in 1911 the two men tramped from Kangaroo Point (Bellerive, on the eastern side of the Derwent) down to Droughty Point, "the way of many of my boyhood days". They climbed Kunanyi/Mount Wellington to the pinnacle and spent two nights at the Springs Hotel, part way up the mountain (sadly burned to the

The Springs Hotel, Mount Wellington, 1910
Photographer: James Chandler
Libraries Tasmania NS869/1/357

ground in the 1967 bushfires). From an upper window they watched the "glory of the sunrise", looking across to Sorell and Frederick Henry Bay. In 1948 Bridges looked back on the moment, and wrote:

> The beauty and wonder of the island rolled on me, possessed me, and possesses me yet. We were talking and talking – life, Australia, journalism, literature; always we planned; always we hoped. We were worshipping life, the island, the sun.

If you are thinking what I think you are thinking, then no. Schuler returned Bridges's friendship but, as Mark Baker makes clear in his 2016 biography of Schuler, he was thoroughly heterosexual and Bridges knew it. This could have been one of those passionate platonic friendships between men, but in 1990 I thought, and I still think, that Bridges was absolutely in love with Schuler.

After brilliant success as the *Age*'s correspondent during the Gallipoli campaign in 1915, Schuler enlisted for active service but was killed in northern France in June 1917. His last letter to Bridges ended: "Keep remembering". Schuler's photograph was another that Bridges cherished always, and indeed he had it reproduced in his 1948 memoir, but Bridges himself was no Peter Pan. He had to carry on facing the disappointments that life inevitably brings, and he was not stoic. In his fifties, living with his sister Hilda back at Woods, he felt the loneliness deeply and became a demanding, querulous, self-pitying man who drank too much.

He did still have many friends, though, and in 1938 he began corresponding with Ted Turner, an amateur painter whom he met through their membership of a Melbourne literary society known as the Bread and Cheese Club. Bridges was only a distant member because he rarely left Tasmania by then, but he took a fancy to Turner and found great entertainment in the younger man's letters, which reminded him of his own Bohemian days in Melbourne. Bridges heaped affection and confidences on Turner, requested a photograph and was delighted with it. He was cross if Turner delayed writing and begged him to visit Tasmania ("Ted old son ... I wish I had your friendship – near me!"), but Turner never did.

The two men met only once, in April 1940 when Bridges made the trip to Melbourne, but Bridges went home hungover and with a bout of influenza. He admitted to Turner that the trip had been "a series of indiscretions". What exactly that meant I couldn't tell, and their correspondence declined later that year.

* * *

Did I indulge in absurd speculation in my thesis about domineering mothers and emasculated fathers? No, but it was impossible to ignore the breakdown of the marriage of Samuel and Laura Bridges in 1907, when Roy was twenty-two. Samuel was pleasure-loving and extravagant, and eventually the house in north Hobart where Roy and his sisters were brought up had to be sold. Of Laura, Samuel apparently said that she "may as well" live with Roy because "it's plain she'll never be happy without him".

Laura managed the household while Hilda became her brother's amanuensis, writing or typing all his novels from his rapidly scrawled sheets. Roy supported them all financially, although Hilda earned an income as a musician and fiction writer. Only now does it occur to me that there might have been an understanding among the three of them, tacit one would think, that Roy would never marry. Before Laura died in 1925 she begged Hilda, "Whatever happens, look after Roy," which Hilda did. She never married.

Did I scour Bridges's writings for autobiographical clues to his sexuality? Yes, because no-one warned me against mistaking writers for their characters, and anyway there was so much material to work with. Convicts, bushrangers, and the endeavours of the early colonists to establish a free and democratic society on Van Diemen's Land: Bridges wrote obsessively on these themes for years.

Novel after novel, especially in his mature period, features a misaligned relationship between a beautiful, passionate woman and an unsuitable man. A son of the relationship will turn up as a convict in Tasmania, and the plot revolves around whether the mother's folly can be forgiven and her son redeemed by love. Bridges despised hypocrisy and religious intolerance, and his clergyman characters are tormented by unsuitable desires and undone by having to preach Christianity to convicts who are not inherently evil but victims of an unjust society.

Symbolic of society's condemnation of a convict were the physical scars left by flogging, for which Bridges seemed to have a horrified fascination. In his final novel, *The League of the Lord* (1950), the Reverend Howard France sits in his study in Sorell picturing an illicit meeting between a beautiful young local girl and her convict lover, which he knew was occurring at that moment. France is jealous of them both. "[Joan's] eyes are deep blue ... her mouth is red, her hands long and white ... exquisite ..." Further down the page France imagines the couple being caught, which would mean the triangles for young Martin: the "hiss and crack of the lash across strong young shoulders ... red weals ... red flesh ... red running ... red."

Martin himself is deeply ashamed of being a convict and struggles to accept the love offered by his (free) family in Tasmania. He recalls his journey there on a transport ship, hoarded below decks with hundreds of other convicts:

> The faces, the eyes, the voices, the hands; the loathsome, pawing, feeling, gliding, gripping hands ... the squeaking laughter in the obscene dark ... the foul perverted horde that [had] been men and boys ... the brooding, breeding evil, the bestiality, lifelong contamination, incurable, malignant, cancerous.

In 1990 I underlined this passage in my copy of *The League of the Lord* but didn't know how to use it. Now I see it two ways. It could simply be an evocation of Marcus Clarke–inspired Tasmanian gothic. Or it could be evidence that Bridges's many convict characters are studies of profound shame, self-hatred and alienation. In this reading, those convict characters were versions of himself, their alienation his own, and homosexuality his source of shame. Either interpretation is possible.

* * *

Roy and Hilda Bridges returned to Woods in 1935 to fulfill a promise Bridges had made to their uncle, Valentine Wood, who'd died in 1930, to take on the old place. Roy knew that Woods meant more to him than Melbourne: "that I was of this land; that it was stronger than I, and that when it willed it would call me back". Still, brother and sister missed Melbourne terribly, even though overstrain and a nervous dread of noisy neighbours had driven Roy to the brink of a breakdown. It might have been in these years that the Imperial Hotel incident occurred. Did it? Bridges disliked Hobart, but if it was casual sex he needed, where else could he go? And yet, if the Imperial was a known place for gay men to meet, the police would surely have been there too. Put that way, the incident seems unlikely.

Bridges had a heart condition which worsened in the late 1940s, and he had a chronic smoker's cough. He refused to go to Hobart for tests and hated doctors visiting from Sorell. One doctor threatened to have him certified to get him to hospital. "He implied my not liking women about me in such treatment was an abnormality," Bridges grumbled to a friend. The burden of his care fell as usual on Hilda. Eventually he had to be rushed to hospital in Hobart anyway, and he died there in March 1952, aged sixty-six. Hilda stayed on at Woods for many years until she moved to a Hobart nursing home, where she died in 1971.

I never spoke with Bridges's family about his possible homosexuality because I was relying on them for recollections and photographs. I drove out to Woods for a final polite visit to give them a copy of the thesis, and after that, unsurprisingly, I never heard from them again. My research had not included any reading on the ethics of biography, so instead I learned it the hard way. I'd gained the trust of my subject's family only to betray that trust in the end. However, this time – for this essay – I contacted a relative a generation younger and did have a frank conversation about Roy Bridges. There is nothing new to say about that except that Bridges left a complex personal legacy that is still being felt.

Some people blame homosexuality among male convicts for the long shadow of repression and homophobia in Tasmania that delayed gay law reform until 1997. Perhaps. Such a thing would be hard to prove and, in any case, what is "proof"? What constitutes "evidence" of a queer life? When found, how do we assess its significance? The important thing is to not shrink from the task, because with patience and honesty we might still open up some of these painful histories to the light.

Memories, $2 Each

Passing through Oatlands, in the Tasmanian midlands, one day in 2022 my brother Paul and I stopped at an antiques and collectibles shop in the main street. Oatlands is renowned for its Georgian sandstone buildings – eighty-seven, which is apparently the largest number in any village setting in Australia – but this was not one of them. It was probably once a large general store.

Undistinguished on the outside, the interior is a palace of dreams for collectors and retro lovers. Furniture, porcelain, ceramics, glassware, jewellery, ornaments, mechanical components, photographs, lamps, clocks, books, radios, tools, baubles, knick-knacks and gimcracks beyond description. My brother came away with a late-1950s Philips three-speaker valve radio in a cabinet of hand-crafted Italian walnut veneer. Worth a fortune when new, he told me, bought by the sort of people who kit themselves out with elaborate home theatre systems today.

I love to fossick but I rarely buy anything because it's usually enough just to be surrounded by old stuff. But I stopped in front of a small wooden box full of postcards; anything with old handwriting always catches my eye. I glanced at a few. In September 1915 Auntie Daisy received birthday love from Bert and Dave. Bernard from Mangana wrote an undated card to his friend Gilbert in St Mary's: "Have not heard from one another for a long time. How do you like your bicycle ride to school?" Fanny wrote to her Auntie Lily thanking her for the nice photo she'd sent of the twins, adding that Mother was too busy to write but would as soon as she had time.

Here was no cache of love letters or the correspondence of some august family, just snippets from the vanished lives of ordinary people. I asked the shopkeeper how much for the lot? I hoped for a discount, but instead, while I browsed the jewellery and tried not to hover, she counted them out carefully into bundles of fifty. There were 180 altogether, and at $2 each that was $360, more than I could afford. I took fifty. I asked her to hand me any bundle but to include a couple of cards that had particularly caught my eye. Other than that, my selection was entirely random.

* * *

Most postcard collectors collect for the illustration on the front and for the age, rarity and physical condition of the cards. Messages written on the back are of minor interest unless they help date the card. Stamps and postmarks help. On that basis I should be feeling glum about the value of my little collection. A few are postcards sent from holiday destinations and might catch the eye of a collector, but most are greeting cards carrying illustrations of flowers, birds, cute puppies or idealised rural scenes. Most are undated but the designs suggest a decade or so either side of the First World War. Stamps have usually been torn off and some have different prices pencilled on them. Clearly, many in my set have already filtered in and out of other postcard collections.

Here were fifty uncherished leavings from lives long ended, of only minor interest to collectors and, as I have every reason to know in a thirty-year career as a historian and curator, even less to museums, libraries and archives. Context is everything. Without that, items like these carry little obvious research or evidentiary value. So why bother? There are plenty more practical things upon which to drop $100. But fate had chucked these $2 memories my way and was challenging me to make something of them. For someone in my line of work, this feels deliciously transgressive. Can I coax any historical narratives out of material as meagre as this? I select four for deeper investigation.

* * *

I started with the easiest, a postcard that had been sent to a Tasmanian solider fighting in the First World War. Unlike all the others in my set it came encapsulated in a mylar sleeve. Mylar is clear polyester film widely used by libraries and serious collectors because it is inert and will not chemically react with the material preserved in it. Obviously a collector had already noticed that an Anzac association enhances the item's significance. (Isn't that always the way with anything Anzacy?)

The card is dated July 1918, and reads: "Dear Fred, with hearty good wishes for a happy birthday, from your old friend, Joy." Joy had followed the correct procedure for addressing mail to soldiers by including his service number, rank and military unit: "No. 6373 Pte Fred Zantuck, 12th Battalion, Australian Imperial Force, Abroad."

This was enough information for the postcard to find its way to Private Zantuck and yet it never had a stamp, so it must have been included with a letter or parcel. This makes sense. The cost to post items to soldiers was a shilling for every half-ounce (fifteen grams) or fraction thereof. Why spend a shilling to send a single postcard? Thanks to Joy's care with the address, it took me very little time to discover basic details of Zantuck's service, and his life afterwards. Frederick Zantuck enlisted in 1916 and returned in 1919. His cousin Vernon Zantuck also served and returned. The Zantucks were a large family of German stock who had long Anglicised their name from Zantuch, and Fred's and Vernon's fathers had been farming in Tasmania near Colebrook for many years. There are Zantucks still living in the district.

Fred was wounded twice in 1918 by gunshot – the first time on the side of his head and the second in the chest – but on his return to Australia a medical board found he had no disability. In August 1919 he married Irene Kay of Launceston, and in 1920 they took up a soldier settlement block on land apparently surrendered by his father. He died in 1964, having farmed at Colebrook all his life save for those few years at the war. The couple appear to have had only one child, Vanda, born in 1920. Irene died in 1984.

All of these threads can be unravelled by following the clues on the postcard sent to Fred by his "old friend" Joy. But what of Joy herself? Fred cared enough to bring her card all the way home to Tasmania and keep it, but was she a school chum, a girlfriend, or a friend of one of Fred's four sisters? Without a surname she is impossible to trace, and that is so often the way. Men who march off to war leave a far deeper imprint on the historical record than do the women they leave behind.

* * *

Next out of my four was not to be a postcard, but a photographic print. It is a black-and-white studio shot of a little blonde boy aged about three, seated and dressed in shorts and a knitted jumper. By his clothes I would say this was 1920s or 1930s, long past the Victorian era when small boys wore dresses. This gorgeous little cherub is smiling slightly away from the camera, but his open hands are extended towards it as if he is offering something to the viewer. His hands are also blurred: obviously the shutter fell while he was still moving. Perhaps this gesture was a convention in the photography of children at the time, but I have not seen it before.

On the back is no name or date, just a simple inscription in black ink: "To Dear Grand-Father, with love". Grandfather appears to have cherished the boy's offering because the print is in excellent condition, as if kept carefully for years in an album.

If there is no clue as to the boy's identity, there is another path to follow. A photographer's impression is visible in the bottom right corner of the print, and back home in Canberra with a magnifying glass and strong light, I could read it: "Ernest A. Winter, Tasma Studio".

In no time I discovered that Ernest Albert Winter had operated a photography studio in Cattley Street in Burnie, on the state's northwest coast. The business was advertised in the local press from 1911 until at least the mid-1950s, when it was being operated by Winter's sons. Winter owned the prominent building and lived upstairs. In addition to studio photography, he developed film for the public, carried Kodak supplies and sold souvenir booklets of his own views of beauty spots around Burnie and the coast. He was secretary of the Burnie Tourist and Improvement Association and served on the local council.

I enjoyed getting to know Mr Winter, but none of it helps with the story of the little boy other than that he probably lived in the Burnie region and that his parents could afford a studio photograph of him. It was a small shock finding it tossed in with a pile of postcards in a collectables shop in 2022. How could the memory of this adorable child have been discarded like that? And yet how easily it can happen. It might only take a generation or two for people to forget the names and faces of their forebears.

* * *

Finally, there is a pair of cards written from Nellie to Dora. From them we get a vivid glimpse of Nellie's life, but blink and you miss it.

Nellie didn't date her cards and they didn't go through the post. One was a Christmas card published by G. Giovanardi, a postcard importer and publisher in Sydney before the First World War. Nellie wishes Dora a happy Christmas and New Year and hopes to hear from her soon. "We went to the South beach on Wednesday and had great fun. I had two swims." Nellie is busy getting ready for Christmas and will be glad when it's all over. "Now Dora," she teases, "I hope you don't eat too much pudding that day." And she concludes, "I must now get to work again. Ta ta. Best love to all from Nellie. XXXX."

The postcards to Dora
Photographer: Anne-Marie Condé

Nellie covers her other card entirely with writing. She still enjoys making a satisfying curl on the capital letter D for Dora, but she is not cheerful and excited now – she is agitated. She begins by apologising for not having answered Dora's letter earlier but, she says, it was received with letters to Trissie while Trissie was staying with a friend, and Trissie – whoever she was – said nothing about it when she came home. Nellie had only discovered Dora's letter that evening and it had been written the previous September. By then it was January, and Nellie had been wondering why Dora had not been writing.

"No Dora," she continues, "Olive does not write to me now. She did not answer my letter of about 12 months ago." Nor had Allen answered the card and letter she'd sent him the Christmas before last. "I thought you must all have been sick of me." Still, Nellie rattles on that she is just back from a short stay with Edith. Tom left that morning for Sydney, for good he says. Ella and Jean are returning to Kin Kin after a month's visit "down here". She concludes by promising to write again and asks Dora to write soon too.

Fortunately, amidst all that chatter there is one contextual clue: Kin Kin is a small town in southern Queensland, northwest of Noosa. Obviously Nellie lives further south – close to the beach, according to her other card. After a bit of mucking about online I established that in 1912, a couple named Charles and Ella Ferris married and settled in the Kin Kin area and that in 1934, Jean Ferris, presumably their daughter, was living with them. So, mother and daughter must have been the "Ella and Jean" who had come south to visit Nellie.

Such were the little comings and goings of Nellie's life. Poor Nellie. Trissie carelessly (or deliberately?) failed to pass on Dora's letter, and Dora didn't bother to write again. Other friends have stopped writing. And just that day, Tom (a brother?) has left home, possibly for good. I'm embarrassed to have stumbled into this seemingly lonely woman's life but fascinated as well. To try to restore lost connections, to weave scraps and fragments together into a narrative, to restore meaning: I can't help myself, can't not do it.

I wonder: was Nellie a spinster, one of those women we assume were washed up after the First World War with no-one to marry? I recall reading somewhere that in demographic terms, the "man shortage" of the 1920s was a myth, but the loss of even a few men in a small community might have been enough to desolate the futures of the women who might have married them. Alternatively, Nellie could have been a frightful gossip and that would explain why people avoided her. I do think she was one of life's doormats. Look at the verse printed on one of the cards. Titled "Gratitude", it reads:

> Fancy you thinking of poor little me
> I feel just as happy as happy can be
> To know that your thoughts
> Sometimes wander my way
> And I hope that our friendship
> Will last dear for aye.

Would Hallmark publish a card like that today? Of course not. We live in a different age, one that elevates personal growth and self-esteem because, as the L'Oréal ads tell us, "You're worth it!" If self-pity is your issue, talk to your therapist.

Pleasingly, Dora, the recipient of Nellie's cards and perhaps others (I chewed my lip at the thought that I'd left some behind in Oatlands) did keep them. Somehow the cards made the journey to Tasmania, brought by Dora or someone associated with her, and were preserved, or at least not thrown out, until years later when someone bundled up the cards with other unwanted stuff for a secondhand dealer to pick through. Finally, someone – me – bought them and read them and wondered what had happened to Nellie, Dora and their circle all those years ago.

* * *

I love these quiet mysteries and history beyond the walls of museums and libraries. When someone finds newspaper underneath their old kitchen linoleum, they keep it and marvel at how life was "back then". Old bricks with makers' marks are a great find, as is a shoe discovered in the walls of an old house, left by a builder as a lucky charm. Detectorists who find old war medals will take to the internet to find the descendants and return the medals because it feels like the respectful thing to do. Scraps of old letters used as templates in a patchwork quilt make us yearn to piece them together. Secondhand booksellers sometimes collect and share the forgotten notes and scraps they find left in books.

A Latin phrase expresses it perfectly. *Ubi sunt qui ante nos fuerunt*: "Where are those who were before us?" Ah, Nellie, what happened to you?

You're Not Going to *Buy* It, Are You?

I sometimes think of myself as a rag-picker, someone who scours refuse discarded by other people. Rag-pickers, or rag-and-bone men, were a common sight in industrialised towns and cities in the nineteenth century. They walked the streets with carts and sacks into which they would gather all sorts of detritus, literally including rags (sold for making paper) and bones (useful for many purposes, from buttons to fertiliser). There was even a market for horseshoe nails scraped from between paving stones.

Be assured that I don't make a habit of sifting through suburban rubbish bins at night. In my day job as a social history curator I interpret historical material for display in exhibitions, and in that work, an understanding of the context and significance of objects is critical. In my downtime, though, I grub for the bits of history left behind in charity shops, collectables shops and markets. I'm not a collector; I just like being in the presence of old stuff. Fine antique shops bore me because everything in them has already been assessed for its market value. All is tidily identified, with no space for adventure or mystery. I'm drawn to the places where I can be unsettled by orphaned artefacts and random associations. In charity and collectables shops it's up to the customers to establish significance, and they'll do this on the spot through Google searching, but also by drawing on their own imagination and memories.

"Oh, my mum used to have one of those!" is a commonly overheard remark, referring perhaps to vintage Tupperware or a CorningWare casserole dish. I once spotted a glass jug exactly the same as the one my mother used for mint sauce, but I didn't buy it, because really, it was rather ugly. Maybe Mum thought so too, but it was what she had.

Whether or not someone will buy other people's discarded stuff depends entirely on how they reimagine its use and reinvest it with new meaning. Inversion of value is something that the French writer Raymond Queneau had great fun with in his 1967 poem "The Bin-Men Go on Strike":

> it's strike day for the bin-men
> it's a lucky day for us
> we can play ragpicker or peddler
> junk dealer who knows even antiquarian
> there's a little of everything ...

A little of everything. I like that. Suddenly you see a work of art abandoned by some "ignorant philistine": the *Mona Lisa*, is it? Or *The Night Watch*, the *Venus de Milo* or *The Raft of the Medusa*?

Carol Rumens chose "The Bin-Men Go on Strike" for her "Poem of the Week" column in the *Guardian* in April 2023. She suggests that Queneau "conjures art from soiled fragmented images" and, in so doing, simultaneously goes in the opposite direction to reduce art back to rubbish. Who gets to declare what is art and what is not art? And so, I thought when I read the poem, who gets to declare what is history and what not? Anyone, not just a trained historian or curator. Feeling superfluous is very freeing.

* * *

On a trip to Melbourne in June 2023 I was happily playing this game in my head in the Chapel Street Bazaar – one of the largest secondhand markets I've ever seen – when I was brought up short by a commemorative plate, one of those limited-edition ceramic pieces that people collect for display on a shelf or wall. After blinking at it for a few seconds I realised it depicts a moment shortly after the arrival of the First Fleet at Sydney Cove in 1788. A couple of ships lie at anchor, a Union Jack has been hoisted, and convicts and marines are busy rowing barrels of supplies to a small jetty. Someone has pitched a tent, and already a few trees have been felled to create a clearing.

It was priced at $95. Gingerly I picked it up and turned it over. The painting was titled "Ships of the First Fleet, Sydney Cove" and had been commissioned by Westminster Australia (a company specialising in commemorative ceramics, I later learned) for a limited firing to mark the Australian bicentenary in 1988. The original work was painted by maritime artist Ian Hansen.

A little of everything, Chapel Street Bazaar, 2021
Photographer: Edward Condé

Immediately I was taken back to the raucous year-long "celebration of a nation" that was 1988. Most particularly I remember the promotional jingle that planted a twelve-month earworm in our heads:

> Come on give us a hand,
> Let's make it grand!
> Let's make it great in '88,
> Come on give us a hand!

"The road to the Bicentenary was certainly a winding and treacherous one," notes Frank Bongiorno in *The Eighties: The decade that transformed Australia* (2015). His remark makes me wish I had been paying more attention to the swirl of entangled ideologies going on at the time, but, living in Hobart and wrapped up in my own life, I wasn't. The First Fleet re-enactment did penetrate my world, mainly because the "tall ships", as everyone called them, visited Hobart in early January 1988 for a race to Sydney ahead of the spectacular re-enactment event on the harbour on 26 January. Also on that day in Sydney, a protest was attended by more than 40,000 Indigenous Australians and supporters from across the country. I don't have Indigenous heritage, and I confess with shame it barely registered with me.

Instead, I recall a lot of people running about in period costumes, and the myriad television specials, concerts, books and so on. The official bicentennial logo – a map of Australia in green-and-gold diagonal stripes – was impossible to ignore. It was on everything from caps to coffee mugs to commemorative coins. I thought it would be on the back of this plate too, but no, this was an unofficial production. I put it back on its little stand. It all seemed such a long time ago.

Gradually I started to notice the clutter of other things on the same shelf. A matching hen and rooster in ceramic. A glazed figurine of a cat. A couple of lamps. A decanter and glasses. A bunch of artificial tulips in a vase. A stack of video cassettes topped by a biscuity-looking bust of the Madonna and child.

Tucked in next to the plate was a ceramic bell labelled "4 generations souvenir bell $45", featuring an illustration of four generations of the royal family: the then-Queen, Prince Charles, Prince William and Prince George. The illustration was obviously taken from a photograph of Prince George's christening in 2013, and I discovered later that it had been posed to match a photograph taken in 1894 of the christening of the future Edward VIII. In that photo, Queen Victoria is seated holding the baby prince while the child's grandfather and father (later Edward VII and George V) stand behind. The photographs were taken 119 years apart, but in each the elderly female monarch is flanked by three future English kings. Extraordinary when you think about it.

Here then, in this crazy jumble of stuff, was a glorious freewheeling rejection of the power of professional museums to control the language of acquisition and display; a laugh-out-loud moment for a curator on a day off. This is what I turn up for in collectables shops.

The centrepiece was the commemorative plate, innocently inviting the viewer to remember the earliest days of white settlement on this continent. The flag seen on the right had been hoisted at an informal ceremony on 26 January 1788 at which Captain Arthur Phillip, having decided that this was the best place to establish the colony, had gathered a small party of officers and others to drink to the success of the new colony and the health of their king, His Majesty George III. And there, depicted on that other useless ceramic thing – the bell – are George's smiling descendants. There's his little namesake, who will one day (presumably) be crowned George VII. The god they all worship makes an appearance too, on an altar of video cassettes, also as a babe in arms.

A little of everything, as Raymond Queneau puts it, but at its heart there was a yawning absence. "Ships of the First Fleet, Sydney Cove" doesn't depict a single Indigenous person – not one of the Eora people who had cared for that coast for tens of thousands of years before Phillip's men planted the Union Jack there. There is nothing to suggest the complex meeting of two vastly different cultures, none of what

Inga Clendinnen, in *Dancing with Strangers* (2003), called "hugger-mugger accidents, casual misreadings, and unthinking responses to the abrasions inevitable during close encounters of the cultural kind". Certainly there is no hint of violent dispossession. This was a 1988 view of 1788, and all the manufacturer wanted was to make money by producing something that people would be happy to display in their living rooms.

Actually – and this is no surprise in a collectables shop – I was surrounded by numerous examples of complex cultures and histories reduced to toy-like simplicity for domestic consumption. Walking about with fresh eyes I noticed a moustached Mexican doll in a sombrero, several black baby dolls (one of them ludicrously dressed in a grass skirt), some "golliwogs", some "African" masks and a couple of very choice examples of "Aboriginalia".

Some mid-twentieth-century kitsch is genuinely good fun. It makes us smile, and sometimes generates fresh inspiration for artists and other creatives. But look again at what lurks. While these objects tell us little about the cultures their makers sought to represent, they tell us a great deal about ourselves. Our ignorance, our insularity and casual racism take artefactual form and, over time, fall to the bottom to form a giant, heaving slurry of *stuff* that we often just don't know what to do with.

* * *

"You're not going to *buy* it, are you?" my son Harry queried when I told him about the commemorative plate that evening. Of course not, I said, although the thought had crossed. But to do so would enhance the market for this kind of thing and would, I thought, make me complicit in the artefact's reductive re-enactment of the past. To own it would be to accept its message. For the price of $95 I would be rejecting Clendinnen's warning that the people of the past are more than "just ourselves tricked out in fancy dress".

So I walked away. The plain truth of it is that I'd be embarrassed to own the plate myself and I'm hoping that a public museum somewhere has acquired one, so that I can shuffle responsibility from the personal to the collective. I did some searching through various online collection databases but had no success with this particular item, although that's not to say it's not out there somewhere.

The 1988 bicentenary seems to be well represented in public collections generally, which is heartening. It shows that, after all, there is a role for publicly funded museums (and libraries and archives) to preserve evidence that disturbs and unsettles our comfortable views of ourselves and our history. It is a job too important to be left to chance. At some point, bin-men and curators all need to get back to work.

Charles Darwin, George Frankland and Me

I had been introduced to Mr Frankland, the Surveyor-General, and these days I was much in his Society. He took me on two very pleasant rides and I passed at his house the most agreeable evening since leaving England.

Charles Darwin wrote this in his diary in Hobart in February 1836, towards the end of his five-year journey with HMS *Beagle*. The agreeable evening was that of his twenty-seventh birthday.

Beagle had anchored in Hobart on 5 February after a six-day journey from Sydney, and while it had encountered fine weather out of Sydney, latterly the conditions had been "very cold and squally". As the ship entered Storm Bay, Darwin discovered, as have so many other mariners before and since, that the weather there "justified this awful name". Ill-humoured after a messy run up the Derwent, Darwin's first excursions ashore left him feeling that the town was "very inferior" to Sydney.

However, after a few days, Darwin began to change his mind. The climate was damper than in Sydney, he noticed, and the land more green and fertile. Agriculture was flourishing. "The cultivated fields looked very well and the gardens abounded with the most luxuriant vegetables and fruit trees." He and his assistant, Syms Covington, paid sixpence each to catch a steamboat across the river to Kangaroo Point and walked around present-day Bellerive as far as Howrah. With the help of a guide he and Covington climbed to the summit of Kunanyi/ Mount Wellington, from which they had a clear view of the mountains to the north. To the south, the land and the river were laid out for them "like a map". After that, the young scientist was better able to appreciate the geology and natural history he observed on the "pleasant rides" he was taking with Mr Surveyor-General Frankland. George Frankland took him to the limestone quarry at what is now the top end of Burnett Street in North Hobart, to Long Beach at Sandy Bay, and to Ralph's Bay on the eastern side of the river near present-day Tranmere.

Amidst these exertions Darwin found time to enjoy some society. Having dined with the solicitor-general, Alfred Stephen, at his magnificent house on Macquarie Street, Darwin wrote to his sister Catherine that with a party of Stephen's most "intimate friends" he heard a concert of "first rate" Italian music. And yet his fondest memory was dinner with the Franklands – George and his wife, Anne – at their house, Secheron, on the river at Battery Point, a little south from the centre of Hobart. We have no record of the other guests that night but there must have been something especially mellow in the Franklands' hospitality that soothed Darwin's soul after so much travel. Once home, he never left Britain again over the course of his long life, but many years later he confided to a friend that emigration to Tasmania was still "his castle in the air".

I love to imagine that "pleasant evening" at Secheron in the summer of 1836 when, after dinner, the gentlemen might have stepped out together through the French windows to take the air. As they walked through the garden, they might have gazed across the river and up at the southern stars. Other than their voices, the only sound would have been the water lapping the stones at the little beach below the house.

* * *

George Frankland was a most amiable man, well travelled, educated in arts and sciences, cultured, urbane. An officer with the British army, he arrived in the colony in 1827 as first assistant surveyor, having previously served as a surveyor with the British army in India. He was promoted to surveyor-general the following year.

Lieutenant-Governor George Arthur directed Frankland to make a trigonometrical survey of the island, and Frankland took this as a broad brief "to observe and record every remarkable fact connected with the Natural history of the island". Frankland was more excited by the opportunity to explore and survey unknown parts, and to make scientific observations and collect specimens for his own museum, than the "plodding work", as he called it, of surveying properties for settlers. His map showed the locations of new counties and parishes and the position of each settler's grant (including, quite prominently, his own grant in Hobart). For the next twenty years this was the most authoritative map available.

Frankland's detractors grumbled that he was never in his office but instead might be found in the studio of Thomas Bock, in Campbell Street, where the convict artist was drawing his likeness. Frankland himself was a good amateur artist, although little of his work has survived. He had a natural gift for obtaining the trust and affection of women. One newly arrived immigrant, Elizabeth Fenton, found him so "kindly and obliging" that after only half an hour's acquaintance she felt as if she had known him ten years. By contrast, his relationship with the lieutenant-governor was often tense and it was said that Frankland only "kept in well" with Arthur because Mrs Arthur "could not do without him in her parlour". Arthur's appointment ended in 1836 and when the new governor, Sir John Franklin, arrived in Hobart, there at the wharf was George Frankland with an enormous bunch of flowers for Lady Jane, the governor's wife.

Frankland took his job seriously and was good at it, but the grand scheme of his life in the 1830s was the development of his own estate at Battery Point. He dreamed of a beautiful house on the river, built to his own design, small but joyously formed, and set in seven acres of gardens and parkland. He named his property Secheron after a town of that name on Lake Geneva in Switzerland, which he had apparently visited.

Building commenced with the section known as "the Gothic cottage", so named because, by some whim of Frankland's, several of the windows were shaped like those of a Gothic cathedral. The main part of the house was more conventional – single-storeyed, but with a basement with windows looking over the garden. Instead of a flat frontage, Frankland designed a protruding central bay window, and it is this feature – this imaginative interruption to Georgian austerity style – which I believe gives the house its particular beauty. Around the house Frankland laid out "pleasure gardens", as he called them, including fruit trees and a network of paths along which he and Darwin might have strolled that night in 1836. By no means would Frankland allow a carriage drive to sully the view between his front windows and the water. There was to be no grand front entrance at Secheron. Instead, the drive was laid out behind the house, with visitors expected to make their entrance across a plain courtyard.

With their three children, the Franklands moved into Secheron in 1834, but George had only a few years to enjoy it all before he died suddenly in December 1838, aged only thirty-eight. By then he was in financial strife, having borrowed heavily to improve the Secheron estate. He had offered it for sale but, failing to find a buyer, had been arranging to lease it when he died. Anne inherited everything, sold her husband's possessions, and moved with her children back to England. Secheron did not sell until 1845. The veranda and balustrade which today lend so much character to the building were added in the 1850s by a later owner, but I hope that Frankland, with his eye for beauty, would have approved. With these additions the house seems to embrace the river, and gather into itself a perfect harmony of water, sunshine and stone.

* * *

In 1956 Secheron came up for sale. It had changed hands many times since the Franklands' day, of course, but except for some essential modernisation it had been altered remarkably little. It was bought by my grandparents, George and Catherine (Kitty) Condé. They occupied the main part of the house and rented out the Gothic cottage – which in the 1930s had been turned into a separate residence – to my newly married parents. My family owned Secheron only for ten years but that decade saw the arrival of my two brothers and me, the youngest. There are a couple of photographs me taken in the garden on the day my parents brought me home from hospital. And I have a memory of another one of me when I was a bit older, a smiling toddler in a white dress sitting by a window, one plump little hand resting on an ancient, convict-made window frame. Did I imagine this? Several years ago when visiting my brother in Hobart, I hunted through the family albums but I couldn't find it.

As I was growing up, my parents would mention Secheron occasionally, just casually, if it came up in conversation. (Always they pronounced it "Seshr'n", not "Secheron"; that seemed to be the accepted pronunciation.) To them it was just a time in their lives which was past. Occasionally on a Sunday afternoon we might drive past for a look, but we could never go in because it was owned by someone else. They indulged me with stories if I asked, which was often because I was furious with them for having left Secheron while I was still much too young to retain any memories of my own.

I could have grown up in my very own creaky old mansion, like a museum except that you get to live in it. And it had a *cellar!* In the adventure stories and Gothic romances I read as a child and teenager, everyone had an attic or a cellar or a tower room, and of course there would be treasure maps and buried keys and all that sort of thing. There were no adventures to be had in the ordinary suburban houses we lived in after Secheron.

I didn't learn of the Darwin connection until I was a university student. Charles Darwin – the great scientist, whose theory of evolution through natural selection changed the course of human thought – had dined in *our house*. He had stepped across the same courtyard where my brothers later played with a pedal car and a toy aeroplane. My first steps could have been taken in the same drawing room in which the young explorer had entertained the company with tales of his adventures in Patagonia and the Galapagos Islands. It's an extraordinary thought, but I keep it in the back of my mind like a treasure in a box, to be brought out and wondered at occasionally, then put away.

It's Secheron itself, really, I long for. We moved away when I was less than two years old, and I'm eternally dissatisfied with borrowed memories. It is part of my story but it's not my house. Who has not wondered about the house in which they grew up, and returned to it perhaps only to lurk outside on the street because that's all you can do? It's worse if the house is no longer there, although in my case the house is very much still there. In 1966 my family had trouble finding a buyer and eventually the state government stepped in, reluctantly, and bought it. It was leased for many years to various community

Catherine Condé at Secheron House, early 1960s
Author's collection

groups, some of which did not treat the old place kindly, until eventually it was sold back into private hands. It has been well looked after ever since by people with far greater financial means than my family could ever have mustered.

Very good. But where does that leave *me*? Still knocking, still peering in, never able to enter. Max Dupain photographed Secheron for a book he published in 1963 on Georgian architecture, and I have his two superb images open at my desk as I write. I was not around in 1963, but how easily I can imagine my mother shooing away her two clever, curious little sons to leave the great photographer to his work. Often I think about the enormous risk my grandparents took – in their sixties, for heaven's sake! – to buy the place. True, a lot of Tasmanians live in old houses with rich histories, but back in the 1950s no-one else was bold enough to open their own house for public visitation, as George and Kitty did.

* * *

My grandparents were not Tasmanian but had moved from Brisbane to Hobart in 1936, my grandfather having gained a promotion within the Commonwealth public service. They lived in rented houses until a legacy from my grandmother's brother allowed them finally to buy. By the late 1940s they were pleasantly accommodated in a new house in Seaview Avenue, Taroona, a riverside suburb seven kilometres south of Hobart. This would have seen them to the end of their days in perfect tranquillity, but when Secheron came on the market, my grandmother had to have it.

I don't remember Kitty but by all accounts she was an energetic and gregarious woman, and as her children grew up she began to cast around for new activities to fill her time. Her latent adventurous spirit had been awakened by the unexpected acquisition of a car. Her brother's legacy included a 1940 Plymouth, in as-new condition because it had been hardly driven during the war. It had to be shipped all the way from Brisbane, but once this magnificent creature arrived both my grandparents declared a reluctance to learn to drive. Instead, my father, aged seventeen, was appointed chauffeur, and he loved it. Henceforward my grandparents no longer had to rely on trains but could explore their adopted state at will. Theirs was the natural curiosity of outsiders, urban people looking for a day out in the country. Not having grown up in Tasmania, they had no family ties going back generations and knew nothing of local lore or legend. The still-prevalent embarrassment of having had a convict in the family was no concern of theirs. There was no skin in that game for them at all.

And so, on a Sunday morning, Kitty would wrap freshly baked sausage rolls into a tea towel and pack them into a wicker basket along with a thermos of tea, and they would all set out. Even the family dog, Tessa, was a motoring enthusiast. Their trips took them across the state, and eventually the Plymouth had to be replaced by a series of more economical vehicles, including a Triumph Mayflower. My oldest brother, Paul, remembers that in this, the family thought little of a drive to Burnie and back in a day. Up and down they went along the old two-lane, winding midland highway in a car happiest at forty-five to fifty miles per hour, pedal to the metal at sixty-five.

Kitty now fully indulged her interest in local history. Stopping to buy fruit and vegetables from roadside stalls was a perfect way to strike up long conversations with property owners, and she could not pass a country churchyard without pausing for a look. She would race across to study the headstones, utterly undeterred by long grass, thistles and the possibility of snakes. She owned copies of E.T. Emmett's *Tasmania by Road and Track* and Michael Sharland's *Stones of a Century*, both published in 1952 and classics of Tasmanian travel literature. Sharland's book, illustrated with his own elegiac black-and-white photographs, was a plea for the preservation of Tasmanian colonial buildings before they were lost forever.

Secheron, therefore, was to be Kitty's own slice of history. Her project was to open the house to paying visitors, and Secheron would become one of the first publicly accessible historical houses in Tasmania. George was less keen, but because the purchase was financed partly out of her capital he went along with it. Both were amateurs at historical preservation, but so were most people at that time because there was then no body of professional knowledge on how to interpret heritage places, although the significance of Tasmania's Georgian architectural heritage was at last becoming apparent.

Battery Point, where Secheron is located, has maritime, commercial and domestic heritage stretching back to the earliest days of the colony, and the 1950s was precisely when the suburb was transitioning from being merely "old" to becoming "historical". Economic stasis had been a natural (if unintended) preserver in Tasmania, but after the Second World War some unthinking demolitions in the name of "progress" had at last begun to awaken concern in educated circles. My grandmother did not move in these circles and she was not an activist. It's impossible to imagine her calling a meeting or circulating a petition. She had little secondary education, and after she married never took a paid job as far as I know. And yet there she was, a pioneer in her own way, quietly pursuing her goal while debates about the future of Tasmania's past whirled around her.

Fortunately, there were a few precedents for what she was doing. There was Entally, a 21-room house built in the 1820s in Hadspen, south of Launceston, purchased by the state government and opened to paying visitors in 1950. In 1960, after an earlier failed attempt, a Tasmanian branch of the National Trust was formed in order to rescue a historical house in Franklin, also near Launceston, known as The Hollies. This house opened in 1961 as Franklin House. Closer to hand was Narryna, on Hampden Road in Battery Point, dating from 1836. It was run by a board of trustees and opened in 1957 as the first folk museum in Australia.

From visiting these houses, Kitty would have formed her own ideas about how to present Secheron and conduct her tours. She must have noted that the dilemma with historical houses is deciding which era in their long histories to present and interpret for visitors. At Secheron there was no original furniture, although Paul remembers an old trunk in the house inscribed "Geo. Frankland" (which must have been a loan from someone because it certainly did not come with us when we left in 1966). I don't know if Kitty knew of Charles Darwin's connection with the house but my parents seemed to be unaware of it, so I assume not.

Kitty could not afford genuine colonial furniture but sourced whatever she could from antique shops to fit out the house in an amorphous nineteenth-century style. She greeted visitors in a period costume she made herself, complete with cape and bonnet. Morning and afternoon tea, which she prepared herself, were available at an additional cost. Her interest in history was genuine, but I imagine she also enjoyed playing the chatelaine.

Tours also took in the front garden, which was my grandfather's domain. He planted trees, arranged flowerbeds and replaced the crumbling front steps with new ones, which he concreted himself in a gracious curve emulating the elegant latticework on the veranda supports. Ironically for someone whose house was open for public inspection, George didn't like strangers. Visitors searching for the front door sometimes assumed he was the gardener and would ask for directions. George never disabused them but sent them on their way with a kindly wave. How my father loved to tell that story!

Kitty's Secheron would have reflected the middle-class values of the small number of Tasmanian citizens in the 1950s who were interested in historical preservation. Probably she would have mentioned to visitors that the house was convict-built, but there would surely have been no reference at all to the island's first inhabitants. It would have been much safer to point to the house's eighteen-inch-thick walls, its cedar shutters, architraves and doors, and its Huon pine veranda. For context she probably drew on a book by respected local historian Amy Rowntree: *Battery Point Today and Yesterday*, published in 1951. Amy was a retired teacher and a member of a prominent Battery Point family. She lived across the road from Secheron with her two sisters: Fearn, an artist specialising in Battery Point's old buildings, and Millicent, at one time the secretary of the Battery Point Progress Association. All were active in the establishment of the Narryna folk museum, and I'd be astounded if Kitty did not become very thick with the formidable Misses Rowntree as soon as she moved in.

My grandparents had no government support in their endeavours other than the occasional promotional assistance from the state tourism department. And while Secheron's architectural significance was well understood – in 1946 the Royal Society of Tasmania identified it as "probably the best specimen of early colonial architecture in the Hobart district" – it never quite gained the status of other historical houses. Secheron was not as big, having only about five displayable rooms and a cellar, and by the 1950s its seven acres of gardens and park had long since been subdivided and sold, leaving the house squeezed on three sides by mean little suburban plots. A newly constructed road, Clarke Avenue, cut it off from its water frontage. Without the spacious aspect that we tend to expect of gracious old mansions, photographers and sketch artists have had to work from awkward angles close to the house or settle for less interesting views of the rear courtyard.

Just as more Tasmanian historical houses were being publicly acquired and opened to visitors – Runnymede in New Town is another notable example – Secheron slipped back into private ownership. Today it resides quietly behind a hedge so high few passers-by would even know it is there.

* * *

Kitty died suddenly at Secheron in 1966, aged seventy-six, and I like to imagine George Frankland waiting at the pearly gates to greet her with a bunch of flowers. He of all people would have applauded the glorious, crazy risks she took with Secheron, just as he had done.

However, without her, Secheron was impractical to manage, and my family sold up. The public tours hadn't included my parents' flat, but they must still have been a trial for them. Mum once told me that standing in the kitchen, she would hear people saying, "Oh! Look

Paul Conde (standing) and Mark Conde, Secheron House, c. 1963
Author's collection

at that lovely white geranium! I'm sure they won't mind if I just ..."
Eventually there was nothing left of the plant my mother had grown so proudly. White geraniums were unusual then, she told me. I think she was lonely at times in those early years of her marriage, and she made me sad with her story about the selfish horrible people who took from her this little thing she was trying to create. Now I wish I could make it up to her and buy her a white geranium that no-one could ruin.

Anyway, my parents' flat was too small for the five of us and it was becoming decrepit. The roof leaked and once, when Paul was little, a section of the old lath and plaster ceiling in our kitchen fell off and narrowly missed him. No-one wants to live like that, I can see that now. Paul tells me that among the debris our parents found a seashell. It was probably an oyster shell swirled into the mortar used to build the house, a common practice in early colonial days. Mum and Dad kept the shell for years until somehow it was lost.

How I would have treasured that shell. I could have turned it over in my fingers and imagined its existence linked to mine, of how a home for a sea creature became part of our home. The shell would have whispered to me that yes, it was there, and I was there, and I belong.

A Rainy Day in Hobart

Scrolling through Facebook one evening I came across the photograph overleaf, posted by a member of a Tasmanian history group I follow. She noted that it comes from the State Library of Tasmania but believed its date and location are unknown. Within three minutes of the initial post, two members of the group had commented on top of each other to say the photo was taken at the corner of Liverpool and Elizabeth streets, Hobart, looking up what is now Elizabeth Mall towards the GPO clock tower on the left. That's how quick and attentive people are in groups like this. And they were correct; I know the place perfectly well. I don't live there any more, but it is my home town.

Old photographs are posted in this group several times a day and each attracts many comments, sometimes dozens. This is just one local history group among countless others on Facebook and other social media platforms. Nostalgia is the main theme, certainly, but with every post, comment and share, memories are stimulated and connections with place and community are enacted.

Recollections are often detailed and intricate. Concerning the date of the rainy-day photograph, someone suggested the women's coats indicate late 1950s. "A bit earlier I think," came a swift reply. "By the mid–late 1950s hemlines had risen a few inches to a bit below the knee. I remember them well from my teenage dressmaking days!" Others leapt in to name the makes of the cars, the consensus being that the one in the foreground is an Austin A40 Devon, although a few people suggested a Hillman Minx. "I immediately could smell the upholstery," said one. "Go Dad!"

Still others noticed the banks. People love to reminisce about banks. "What happened to the beautiful old bank on the corner?" someone asked. It's still there, came a reply, now a branch of the National Australia Bank, but had not displayed the correct time for a while. The Hobart Savings Bank on the extreme right of the image has been

Elizabeth Street, Hobart, 1953
Libraries Tasmania AB713-1-2160

pulled down and replaced with what one commenter described as a "modern monstrosity". Someone else claimed to still have a pink bankbook from there with a few pounds in the account, but: "I suppose the government has pinched that." This person remembered being interviewed by the manager there for a home loan, $20,000 over twenty-five years at 6 per cent. "Real service back then by real people, all those tellers. We have lost so much."

By this time I was thoroughly engrossed in the world of this photograph. I sent it to my two brothers. Yes, that's an Austin A40, said Paul, and the car with the smashed-up grille in the centre of the photograph is a Chevrolet ("1939 I think"). He noticed the traffic lights, which I had missed, and how the pedestrians are wearing titfers. Hats, that is. (I had to look that up.) Mark remembered the Kodak store still trading in the 1970s. "Mind you, I remember when Hobart had half-a-dozen good photo/camera stores," he added. As a keen photographer himself, he appreciated the mood and story in the photograph. It's harder than it looks to take pictures that do that. For me the main feature is the GPO clock. Our grandfather worked in that building, and I picture him glancing out the window at that very moment, hoping the rain might have eased in time for his bus ride home.

I like to know the origins of things, so I sought out the photograph's descriptive information at the Libraries Tasmania. It does have a fairly precise date, May 1953. (So, the Facebook commenter knowledgeable about 1950s hemlines was right.) It is one of a series of about 12,000 images made between 1951 and 1973 by the Tasmanian Education Department. Hats off to the library staff for their work to preserve and digitise this series; it's magnificent. The photos cover a wide range of subjects other than schools and education, suggesting that the department's photographers could be called on for a variety of assignments. Our rainy-day photograph shows that they might have also filled the end of a roll on the way back to the office with whatever took their fancy.

Mark was right, it's the mood of the photograph that is captivating. Wet streets are eternally interesting for photographers and artists, and this unknown photographer appears to have sheltered under an awning and brought the shutter down just as everyone is too busy getting out of the rain to notice or care. See how they have caught the Chevrolet's crumpled grille just as it swung around the corner towards us? This car has had a "bingle", as my father would say, the sort of thing that could occur on any wet day. Central Hobart was not built for cars, and yet in these postwar years a lot more people could afford them. The result: frustration.

Then there's the woman on the right, who draws our gaze as she walks briskly away from us into the frame. With her reflection shimmering up from the pavement, she turns provincial Hobart into a scene John le Carré could have conceived. The cut of her coat is pure 1950s. Clothes rationing is out, Christian Dior's New Look is in, and this woman can afford the latest modes. Other women appear to be making do with their older things. The woman with the basket crossing the street, head down against the rain: she could have been wearing that severe jacket and skirt since the 1930s. She'd be about our grandmother's age, I should think, part of a generation for whom frugality was a necessity and later a habit.

The more I look at the photograph, the deeper I fall into a liminal state between connection and disconnection. I know this place, and yet I don't. I belong, and yet I don't. I think it's the raindrops bouncing up off the road that gives the image its perpetual drama. Where will all that water go? In Hobart, it goes into the Hobart Rivulet.

* * *

Autumn is when the rivulet is most prone to flooding. In June 1954, thirteen months after our photograph was taken, flash floods forced several feet of water into the basement of O'Conor's shoe shop. You can see the shop sign in the photograph. Staff working there to save the stock might have drowned if the floor-level windows had given way. There had been bad floods in 1923 and 1947, but the 1954 floods were said to be the worst in a hundred years.

The rivulet emerges on the slopes of Kunanyi/Mount Wellington and runs through present-day Fern Tree and South Hobart. Reaching the city, it ducks underground and up again a few times before disappearing for a kilometre or so directly under the CBD. (In 2016 the rivulet wall was breached during building works, causing more than $15 million in damage to the Myer department store and several retailers in the adjacent Cat and Fiddle Arcade.) Then it comes up for air for a short stretch parallel to lower Collins Street, disappears, and finally meets the River Derwent at an outlet north of Macquarie Point.

For thousands of years Aboriginal Tasmanians moving seasonally through the Hobart region would have understood the rivulet's moods, and how it connected with other natural watercourses to support animal and birdlife. Then, in February 1804, Lieutenant-Governor David Collins decided that this was the ideal place to establish a settlement. The "Run of clear fresh Water" he found there played a large part in his decision. Efforts the previous year at Risdon Cove, on the eastern side of the Derwent, had faltered partly for lack of reliable clean water.

Collins understood the need to protect the rivulet, and within weeks had issued instructions to the settlers not to pollute it or destroy the "underwood" close to its banks. By 1805 a footbridge had been built across it connecting a bush track leading north, which later became Elizabeth Street. This bridge was replaced in 1816 by a brick structure named Wellington Bridge after the famous duke. Today it is covered over by Elizabeth Street, but a small void protected by a grille affords the curious shopper a reminder of Hobart's earliest days.

The first European settlers quickly learned that although the rivulet could sink to a trickle in the summer, heavy rain or snowfall on the mountain could turn it into a torrent. And this was even before the town authorities decided to alter its course for the first time, in 1825, with what was known as the "New Cut" along a section of lower Collins Street. The New Cut diverted the rivulet towards another creek and sent both of them away from their natural bed, which had been under the present site of the City Hall. Their confluence had formed a silty beach prone to flooding, and the diversion was designed to facilitate land reclamation in support of burgeoning waterfront industries.

Early maps of Hobart show how the rivulet once pursued its own gentle course from the mountain to the river, and how ruthless was the grid of streets imposed on top of it. Over time the rivulet has been diverted, dammed and forced through numerous pipes, tunnels and culverts: controlled and exploited, in other words, for the settlers' convenience. David Collins's instructions to protect the rivulet were ignored, and by the mid-1820s it had become polluted by refuse from humans, animals, tanneries and distilleries. Outbreaks of disease were inevitable. In 1828 the town sheriff reported that the rivulet had become a "receptacle for all the filth and impurity of the town".

The strip along lower Collins Street was the worst, and just as likely to flood as before. It has never been a pretty part of town, as you can see. In high school I had to catch a bus along there, and my moody teenage thoughts were not enhanced by having to stare at a tired old

Hobart Rivulet, 1913
Libraries Tasmania PH30-1-721

watercourse while I waited. Residential housing had all gone by then and I didn't know that these streets used to be known unofficially as "Wapping" after the working-class waterfront area of London. For a hundred years or more, the people of Hobart's Wapping suffered the most from flooding and pollution, as the poorest people often do.

Efforts over many decades to improve the supply and quality of Hobart's water finally culminated in 1895 with the completion of two major reservoirs at the Waterworks Reserve above South Hobart, with a combined capacity of 500 million litres. They still supply Hobart's drinking water.

The rivulet can still rise up in anger. Calamitous flooding in 1960 led to new control measures, but in 2018 the section along lower Collins Street once again turned into a seething and very dangerous torrent. A group of urban geographers noted then that the problem (not unique to Hobart) is that urban planning measures have become disconnected from nature and overlook the ecological functions of watercourses. Built-up areas deprive a city of green spaces that act like natural sponges. It's hard to apply water-sensitive planning principles to a city already built.

* * *

At the end of my meditation on the photograph taken in Hobart in 1953, I returned to the original question: where does all that water go? How do we prevent our cities from becoming alienated from their natural environmental features? The upper reaches of the rivulet are better managed now, but the challenges are real.

If you have fifty-three minutes to spare, hop over to ABC iview and search for *The Platypus Guardian*. The subject of this beautiful documentary is Pete Walsh, a Hobart man who first sought solace at the rivulet after a serious medical diagnosis. He was drawn there to reconnect with something he thought he was losing. Sitting on the bank one day, he was astonished when a platypus emerged from the water and zoomed up to him, wiggling her bill as if she had something to say. He realised that a fragile population of platypuses was managing – against all odds – to call the Hobart Rivulet home.

The more Pete visited the rivulet the more often he saw this zooming platypus, so he named her Zoom. That profound moment of connection inspired in Pete a passion to do what he could to preserve a habitat for these ancient animals, and a whole community of supporters has since joined him. If Zoom has a message, it must surely be to ask us to tread more lightly on this earth.

Ben Chifley's Pipe

I once had the task of combing through a digitised file of letters to prime minister Ben Chifley held by the National Archives of Australia. Clicking away, I noticed one from a man named W.H. Reece, sent in August 1946.

> Would you please send me one of your pipes that you may have laid aside and you will not be likely to be using again. If it should be a bit strong, no matter. I know of a process that will overcome that. I have not been able to get a decent pipe for years.

This was not what I was looking for, but I printed the letter out for a closer look anyway. Mr Reece was an aged pensioner twenty days short of seventy-five years, he said, living alone in New Norfolk, Tasmania. He has raised a family of six daughters and three sons. All of the sons had served in the recent war, he added, with one still with the occupying force in Japan. Reece had "battled for Labour" since he joined the Amalgamated Miners' Association in 1889. "I started in poverty and I'm ending ditto, but I've no regrets and have no apologies to offer for my support of the 'Grand Old Labour Movement'." If Mr Chifley were to visit Hobart during the forthcoming federal election campaign, and if Reece is spared that long, he promises to be in the audience. He is very optimistic that the Chifley government will be returned with a strong majority (it was). "I wish you and your good colleagues all the good luck that wishes can express."

I was busy that day and so, having studied the letter for a few minutes and enjoying a giggle about the pipe thing (what was *that* all about?) I tossed it aside and moved on. Fortunately, the pile I tossed it onto was the "do not throw out under any circumstances" pile, where it stayed until the inevitable desk clean-up several weeks later when, at last, Mr Reece finally had my full attention. This is my favourite thing, the deep study of a single archival record. It could be a letter, a telegram or a bunch of postcards discovered in a junk shop. It is remarkable what can be gleaned from seemingly insignificant clues, especially now that these clues can be run through so many newly digitised sources. Becoming deeply immersed in someone else's life, trying to see the world through their eyes, is my form of meditation.

Why this Mr Reece though? What was it about him in particular that called for this deep attentiveness? Partly it was his surname that guided my hand that day towards the "do not throw out" pile rather than the recycling bin. Growing up in Tasmania I recall my parents talking about the redoubtable Eric Reece, a former long-time Labor premier known as "Electric Eric" because of his ardent support for hydroelectric projects. Surely it had to be the same family. But mainly I was captivated by what I perceived as a yearning on Reece's part to stay connected with the world. It's unintentionally expressed, but it's there. Looking back over his long life, this proud and, I think, lonely man tells of the things that most matter to him: his work, his family and the labour movement. Not only that, he also imagines Labor's next victory even if he is not alive to see it.

And the pipe thing? Chifley made his pipe a signature accessory and was rarely seen without one, but it does seem awful cheek to expect him to simply hand one over on request. Chifley wrote back: "Dear Mr Reece, thanks for your letter ... I am sorry that for the present I haven't a suitable pipe to send you. As you say, good pipes are very scarce these days." (Actually Chifley usually had several on hand, gifts from family and well-wishers.) "I was interested to read of your lengthy support of the Labour Movement. You must have many memories to look back on." And he signed off with best wishes.

Ben Chifley, 1948
National Library of Australia PIC P1474/19 LOC Album 897

Reece didn't get his pipe but I doubt he was disappointed. Pipe smoking was a companionable habit the two men shared but Reece's request, I suspect, was just an opening gambit. It has been said of Chifley that he used the lighting of his pipe to stall a conversation while he thought through a reply. Likewise here, pipe-related preliminaries over, Reece felt perfectly free to address his prime minister as an equal, one Labor man to another. The letter wasn't really about the pipe, and – fair warning – this essay is not really about it either.

* * *

William Henry Reece (often known even in official records as Will Harry Reece) was born in 1872, and he was indeed an uncle to Eric Reece. Fortunately for me, there is a biography of Reece the younger, Jillian Koshin's *Electric Eric: The life and times of Eric Reece, an Australian state premier* (2009). Koshin begins with an examination of the Reece family's working-class origins in mining towns in the northeast and west of Tasmania. The discovery of minerals – gold, silver, copper, tin – in the 1870s brought a sudden and massive economic boom to the colony based on interstate investment, higher export income, higher wages and increased incoming migration. In his 2012 history of Tasmania, Henry Reynolds describes the 1880s as one of Tasmania's "sunniest" decades.

Patriarch Owen Charles Reece established himself as a miner in the 1870s but was frequently on the move looking for work. Koshin is at pains to show how the wealth that enriched investors and beautified the cities rarely trickled down to the poorest folk who had laboured to produce it. Across three generations, even in so-called good times, little changed for the Reece family. Owen and his wife, Jane, had fourteen children but the first three, triplets, died in infancy. Jane died in Scottsdale hospital after her last birth, twins, who also died. She was thirty-eight. Owen was left a widower with nine children to raise; our man Will ("I started in poverty ...") was the eldest. A few brothers down the line was George (later the father of Eric) born in 1909.

The Reeces' lives were characterised by insecure and dangerous work and the strain and expense of constantly moving from one primitive slab-and-shingle hut to another in remote and isolated settlements. Because these clusters of dwellings were expected to be temporary, authorities would rarely invest in public amenities. Close-knit families relied on one other.

Out of these struggles emerged a writer, Marie E.J. Pitt. Originally from Victoria, she was married to a miner, William Pitt, and for about a decade beginning in the 1890s went with him to mining settlements in the northeast and west of Tasmania. They had four children, one of whom died. Scribbling by lamplight, Pitt wrote of "an austere land of mountain gorges of ice and snow, and raging torrents of creeping mist and never-ending rain". The land spoke another language, "superb in its silence, appalling in its melancholy grandeur". Her pen was also driven by anger. This is how she begins her poem "The Keening":

> We are the women and children
> Of the men that mined for gold:
> Heavy are we with sorrow,
> Heavy as heart can hold;
> Galled are we with injustice,
> Sick to the soul of loss –
> Husbands and sons and brothers
> Slain for the yellow dross!

Over another nine bitter stanzas she attacks mine owners, politicians and churchmen for having averted their gaze from the misery right in front of them. "The Keening" was published in 1911 but by then the Pitts had moved to Victoria because William had contracted miner's phthisis. He died in 1912.

* * *

Will Reece, his siblings, nieces and nephews were among the children of the men that mined for gold. All the Reece men became union men. Poetry aside, trade unionism was the practical agent of change, the structure within which to advocate for safer working conditions, better wages and political representation. Reece was a seventeen-year-old apprentice blacksmith at the tin mine in Ringarooma when he joined the Amalgamated Miners' Association. For some reason – and here is where the story gets interesting – he broke away from the family and left the mines behind. His parents were married with Baptist rites but Will appears to have converted to Catholicism, a most unusual thing to do in those sectarian times, and certainly enough to cause a family rift.

From the late 1890s he roamed through several agricultural districts in the northeast and in 1909, at St Mary's, he married a woman named Catherine Cannell. In 1912 they went south to New Norfolk, a town nestling in the Derwent valley thirty-five kilometres northwest of Hobart. The landscape was far kinder than anything Will Reece had known growing up, and here the family settled for good.

Literate, articulate and gregarious, Reece would join anything. He played cricket and football, would swing an axe at a local woodchopping event and was always ready to chair a meeting, MC a church fundraiser or write a letter to an editor about some local grievance. Forced in 1915 to give up blacksmithing because of an accident, he opened a photographic studio; it failed, and he was declared bankrupt in 1921. Clearly this man had bucketloads of self-belief. Twice he stood unsuccessfully for the municipal council; undeterred, he turned to state politics and was a candidate for Labor in the elections of 1919, 1922, 1925 and 1928. He failed each time.

Meanwhile, he became an organiser for the Australian Workers' Union, and here he found his métier. His nephew's biographer noticed uncle Will Reece signing up shearers, shedhands, miners, labourers and roadmen across the state, including in mining centres on the west coast. New heavy-industry projects provided fresh fields for the AWU, and there was Will Reece, visiting the new carbide factory at Electrona in the south and the hydroelectricity works at Waddamana in the central highlands. With regular reports he made himself well known to the readers of the AWU's national paper, the *Australian Worker*.

But the 1930s brought reversals. In 1931 more than a quarter of Tasmanian trade unionists were unemployed because of the Depression, and all the Reece men let their union membership lapse. Will Reece returned to manual labour and in 1934, aged sixty-two, was severely injured in an explosives accident while quarrying for gravel. He sustained burns to his face and temporarily lost his sight. In 1935 his wife died suddenly, leaving him still with a clutch of children and teenagers to raise.

In 1939 Will's fifty-year commitment to the labour cause was celebrated at a special meeting of the New Norfolk branch of the Labor Party. Local MP Jack Dwyer spoke about Reece's work to "uplift" the condition of the masses. Many of the privileges now enjoyed by the workers were due to his efforts, Dwyer noted, and the party was much indebted to him. At about that time Will's nephew Eric was embarking on his own (in his case, spectacularly successful) political career. After failed attempts in 1940 and 1943, Eric was elected Labor member of the state House of Assembly in November 1946. He was in office as premier between 1958 and 1969, and again from 1972 to 1975, and was federal president of the Labor Party between 1952 and 1955.

Eric's formative years had been similar to his uncle's: he'd worked in mines and on farms from his early teens – joined the AWU at fifteen – spent most of the Depression unemployed – got a job at the Mount Lyell copper mine in 1934 – was appointed organiser for the AWU there in 1935. Yet strangely, there does not seem to have been a strong association between uncle and nephew. In his 1946 letter to Ben Chifley, Will could have mentioned Eric as a promising youngster to keep an eye on, but he does not.

Still, Will and Eric Reece – and Ben Chifley of course – were all haunted by memories of hardship, and all strove for the same things: economic growth, full employment, increased standards of living, and social welfare for those who needed it.

* * *

In the latter part of his career, there was nothing in Eric Reece's makeup to prepare him for the social upheavals and cultural shifts of the 1960s and 1970s. He had grown up believing that the state's natural resources – its water, timber and minerals – were there to be used for the common good, and he became infamous for having rode roughshod over opposition to the hydroelectric scheme in southwest Tasmania that was to flood Lake Pedder in 1972–73.

Where some people wept at Pedder's beauty, Eric Reece was belligerent and autocratic. In 1966 he taunted his opponents with the remark that Tasmania's southwest contained only "a few badgers, kangaroos, wallabies, and some wildflowers that can be seen anywhere". (There are no badgers in Tasmania, as Reece would have known perfectly well.) Tough old trade unionists like Reece had known destitution, and were lit with a determination to do more than just overcome personal hardship; they were committed to structural reforms to improve the lives of all working people. By this time, however, there had begun a great grinding of gears in progressive politics as young, idealistic, tertiary-educated people drifted away from Labor to the green movement. While this also happened elsewhere, perhaps the grinding came earlier in Tasmania.

Uncle Will Reece didn't live to see any of this. Perhaps, as promised, he did make it to Hobart in September 1946 to hear Ben Chifley's two-hour campaign speech given to a capacity crowd at the town hall. "The whole country is prosperous," Chifley declared that night. "That is the first ideal we have, and we go to the people on that record."

Labor's election loss in 1949 and Chifley's death in 1951 must have saddened Reece. He died in 1953, I hope with his boots on (so to speak) and his certainties intact.

John Curtin's Potato

Dear Sir, I am sending you a cure for your akes and Pains.

On 9 September 1942, Mr W. Frith, an aged pensioner giving his address as Wattle Flat via Bathurst, sent then prime minister John Curtin a small package containing a potato. So important was this potato that Mr Frith felt obliged to include detailed instructions on its use. The prime minister was to put the potato in his pocket, specifically in his left pocket if he was right-handed. In "a few weaks time" it will get a bit soft, Curtin was told. Take no notice of that but leave it there and it will flatten out "like a half crown", and then go "has hard as a pice of wood". After three years it will "whear away to nothing". And then the prime minister should repeat the process. "While you carrie a Potato in your pocket you will never suffer with any Pains." Frith himself had been doing so for the previous twenty-seven years, he said, and suffered no akes or Pains.

The prime minister's private secretary wrote to Mr Frith acknowledging with thanks – but no further comment – the arrival of the package. Frith's letter was carefully filed with hundreds of other personal and official representations under "Correspondence F" for the year 1942. In 2017, while I was working at the National Archives of Australia, a colleague of mine stumbled with delighted amazement upon the Frith correspondence. John Curtin was a popular prime minister, yes, but to send a *potato* as a gift? There were peals of laughter in the office

John Curtin, Sydney Town Hall, 1942
State Library of New South Wales 9581591

that day, let me say, at the thought of a potato-induced protuberance in the prime ministerial pocket.

When one of us finally got around to doing some actual research, we discovered that carrying a potato in one's pocket was a Victorian-era cure for rheumatism. Exactly how it was thought to work is unclear – folk remedies and superstitions do not admit of much close investigation anyway – but it was commonly believed that the potato had to have been stolen for it to work. (Frith makes no mention of this in his letter to Curtin.) The Pitt Rivers Museum at Oxford University includes a number of withered therapeutic potatoes among its holdings of folkloric material.

So, would Curtin have given the potato cure a try? Could a potato have been a silent witness at the next war cabinet meeting, in Canberra on 21 September 1942? I suspect not because although Curtin's health was poor, rheumatism is not known to have been one of his afflictions. If he knew about Mr Frith's gift – and his staff may well have thought he would enjoy the diversion – Curtin may simply have kept it in his pocket until he could hand it to domestic staff at the Lodge for use in the kitchen. Nothing was allowed to go to waste in those austere times.

I was surprised to learn that folklore and superstition still lingered in 1940s Australia, and I wondered if Frith's offering to Curtin was considered odd at the time. As it turns out, yes, just a little. In late 1942 and early 1943, several major newspapers ran stories poking gentle fun at the weird and wonderful letters and packages Curtin often received. Each of these pieces was essentially the same and probably drew on a compilation of letters (writers' names withheld) offered to the press by Curtin's indefatigable press secretary, Don Rodgers. His aim, I imagine, was to rub some edges off his boss's rather stern public image.

Christians sent religious tracts, widows sent wedding rings (goodness!), a lot of people sent money (which went straight to Treasury), inventors sent war-winning suggestions, and one woman sent a cushion embroidered with the words "God Bless Our Prime Minister".

The public was entertained with excerpts from letters to Curtin from various charmers and crackpots, among whom Mr Frith comes off as comparatively sane. Who knows if a copy of any of this ever reached him at Wattle Flat?

Years later, Frith's words still come back to astonish me yet again with their specificity and conviction. Tempting though it is to dismiss him as a bit of a weirdo, it's good to remember that few of us are completely rational all the time. I keep a bottle of echinacea on hand for when I feel a cold coming on even though the evidence for its efficacy is slender. Which of us has not done something similar? A well-known chain of Australian discount pharmacies devotes several aisles in its enormous stores to complementary medicines and dietary supplements, and people obviously buy them. If we laugh at Mr W. Frith of Wattle Flat via Bathurst, we also laugh at ourselves.

* * *

The other reason I often think of Mr Frith is that he reminds me of when I first met the peasant Bodo during my undergraduate days. I still have my copy of Eileen Power's wonderful book *Medieval People*, which was first published in 1924 and went through many subsequent editions. Power chose six people and wrote a chapter on each to personify ordinary life in the Middle Ages. Bodo is the first. He was a peasant living in the early ninth century on an estate attached to an abbey near Paris, owned by the emperor Charlemagne. Because of Charlemagne's close interest in how his lands were managed, the records are extremely rich.

Power discovered Bodo, his wife Ermentrude and their three children, Wido, Gerbert and Hildegard, in the abbot's estate book. With enormous skill and imagination she presents them to us as living, breathing people. We learn of a typical day in their lives by watching Bodo as he sets out on a frosty morning with his ox for a day's ploughing, little Wido coming along to help. Ermentrude's morning was spent at the big house, where she had to pay the chicken rent (a fat pullet and five eggs), and her afternoon at home weaving cloth. Power goes further, boldly proposing not just what her people did but how they thought and felt about it. Bodo wasn't happy on that cold morning, having to plough the abbot's fields when his own were crying out for attention, but he sang lustily to cheer himself and Wido.

We learn that Bodo and Ermentrude spent Sundays and saints' days singing and dancing to ribald pagan songs, a practice that greatly annoyed church authorities. Frankish Christians such as Bodo still clung to much earlier rites and superstitions, but these the church wisely left alone. Charms were said over sick cattle and incantations over fields to make them fertile. The cure for a stitch in one's side, or any bad pain, was to lay a hot piece of metal next to it and say a charm to draw out the nine little worms that were eating one's bones and flesh. (The sensation of the hot metal probably distracted the mind from the stitch, thus making this cure a mite more rational than Frith's potato remedy.)

If Eileen Power speculated beyond the evidence in conjuring up the inner lives of her medieval people, her thorough immersion in a broad range of sources enabled her to, as she put it, "make the past live for the general reader". She was a pioneering social historian and for her book's epigraph she quotes a famous verse in the book of Ecclesiasticus: "Let us now praise famous men and our fathers that begat us." The problem for many of her fellow historians, she said, was that they had forgotten the fathers that begat us. Her aim was to recognise the "unnamed, undistinguished mass of people, now sleeping in unknown graves", upon whose slow toil "was built up the prosperity of the world".

* * *

John Curtin is absolutely one of those famous men, and William Frith one of the toilers. What can be learned about Frith? If I have my genealogical research correct – and there is some ambiguity in the records – William Thomas Frith was born in the small town of Hartley, in central west New South Wales, in 1869, the son of British migrant parents. His father, Oscar, was a labourer who in 1882 appeared before a magistrate for failing to send thirteen-year-old William to school. Probably the boy's labour was needed at home.

Frith's story can be told only through snippets and in fact we probably know less about him than we do about peasant Bodo. The Friths were living in the Carcoar region in 1904 when Oscar and William were charged with assault; William was found guilty but the case against Oscar was dismissed. In 1907 Oscar, aged sixty-six and still working, was seriously injured and nearly lost an ear when his horse and cart toppled over an embankment. The First World War offered an escape (of sorts) for rural families living on the edge of poverty, but not so much for the Friths. William was too old to enlist, although his younger brother John did scrape in at age forty-four in 1915. John was returned to Australia medically unfit in 1917.

By 1930 their parents had died and the brothers were living in Wattle Flat, a village thirty-two kilometres north of Bathurst. This is the famous region of New South Wales where gold had been discovered in 1851, and Wattle Flat apparently once boasted a population of 20,000. A small renewal of mining activity during the Depression might explain why the Friths were living there, listed as miners ("fossickers" might be more accurate) on the electoral roll. John gave up eventually and "went on the track", but William stayed.

He was apparently unmarried and had no evident involvement in any church, sporting club, trade union, friendly society or any other of those organisations that were the glue that held society together in those times. In 1935 the *National Advocate*, Bathurst's main newspaper, noted that Mr W. Frith of Wattle Flat had been admitted to hospital for "medical attention" (for something beyond the powers of a potato, we assume), suggesting that he did have some standing in the community, but in general he appears to have been a loner.

He must have been paying attention to what was going on in the world, however, or he would not have written to John Curtin. The *National*

Advocate was a left-leaning newspaper (it had future prime minister Ben Chifley on its board of directors) and would have been his main source of news. In its pages Frith could have learned of the Japanese entry into the war in December 1941, its aggression in the Pacific in 1942 and the gravity of Australia's position as a consequence. He could have read Curtin's exhortations to his people to expect that each and every Australian would have to make sacrifices. The paper covered Curtin's appeal to the United States for support and his declarations about the need to reorganise labour and industry, introduce rationing and raise funds through war loans. The *Advocate* backed Curtin throughout. He was one of the "greatest leaders in Australian history", the paper claimed.

Historians have noted how Curtin's background as a journalist helped him craft the messages he needed to gain the nation's support for the unprecedented interventions in social and economic life necessary to win the war. In this he was assisted by press secretary Don Rodgers, but Curtin already had a natural ease with journalists and was frank and informal with them in his twice-daily briefings. He also spoke directly to millions of people in his frequent radio broadcasts, and by adopting a plain and direct style of address came across as a hardworking, humble and honest man.

Not everyone could have afforded a wireless, I suppose. I wonder if William Frith had one in Wattle Flat, or could have joined a neighbour to listen in. If so, back in November 1941, shortly after Curtin became prime minister, Frith might have heard him proclaim that:

> This Australia is a land of cities and golden plains, of great rivers and vast spaces. It is a land in which countless thousands of plain, ordinary men and women have toiled long, mostly for little reward; who sacrificed and who built our heritage. If this heritage was worth *their* lives to build, it is worth *ours* to preserve.

It's almost as if whoever wrote the broadcast script (Curtin? Rodgers?) had read and remembered Eileen Power's Bodo and Ermentrude, those slow toilers who built the prosperity of the world. In any case, rhetoric of that kind was exactly what was needed to inspire people like William Frith, whose family had indeed toiled long for little reward. He may have felt (yes, I am speculating beyond the evidence) that now, at last, there was a place for them in the national story.

The effect of that could have been profound, certainly enough for Frith to decide eventually to devise something out of his own small means, in the form of a curative potato, as an offering back to Curtin. And quite possibly he also gave something that Curtin would have valued much more: his vote. In the federal election of August 1943, Curtin's Labor government defeated the Country–United Australia Party coalition by a landslide. It remains one of the greatest victories in Labor history.

History, as Eileen Power said, is largely made up of Bodos.

Further Reading

The Making of a Miniaturist

John Berger, *Ways of Seeing*, British Broadcasting Corporation and Penguin Books, 2008.

My Brother Clive

Tom Griffiths, *The Art of Time Travel: Historians and their craft*, Black Inc., 2016.

Clive Lord, "The Aboriginal: Our original ugly man", *Mercury*, 18 March 1926, p. 3.

Clive Lord, "Preliminary Note Upon the Discovery of a Number of Tasmanian Aboriginal Remains at Eaglehawk Neck", *Papers & Proceedings of the Royal Society of Tasmania*, 1918, pp. 118–19.

Clive Lord, *Some Tasmanian Days*, Examiner Press, 1926.

Clive Lord, "The Tasmanian Aborigines", Report of the Eighteenth meeting of the Australasian Association for the Advancement of Science, Perth 1925, vol. xviii, pp. 523–24.

Clive Lord, "The Tasmanian Aborigines", in L.F. Giblin et. al, *Handbook to Tasmania, 1928*, prepared for members of the Australasian Association for the Advancement of Science, Hobart, 1927, pp. 14–18.

Stuart Macintyre (ed.), *The Historian's Conscience: Australian historians on the ethics of history*, Melbourne University Press, 2004.

Robert Manne (ed.), *Whitewash: On Keith Windschuttle's fabrication of Australian history*, Black Inc., 2003.

Cassandra Pybus, *A Very Secret Trade: The dark story of gentlemen collectors in Tasmania*, Allen & Unwin, 2024.

The Telegram

Colin Bale, *A Crowd of Witnesses: Epitaphs on First World War Australian war graves*, Longueville Media, 2015.

Hilary Mantel, *A Memoir of My Former Self: A life in writing*, John Murray, 2023.

Michael McKernan, *Australian Churches at War: Attitudes and activities of the major churches 1914–1918*, Catholic Theological Faculty and Australian War Memorial, 1980.

Bart Ziino, *A Distant Grief: Australians, war graves and the Great War*, University of Western Australia Press, 2007.

The Names Inlaid

K.S. Inglis assisted by Jan Brazier, *Sacred Places: War memorials in the Australian landscape*, Miegunyah Press, 1999.

Unquiet Stories from Liffey

Shayne Breen, *Contested Places: Tasmania's northern districts from ancient times to 1900*, Centre for Tasmanian Historical Studies, 2001.

Nicholas Clements, *Black War: Fear, sex and resistance in Tasmania*, University of Queensland Press, 2014.

Lyndall Ryan, *Tasmanian Aborigines: A history since 1803*, Allen & Unwin, 2012.

Rock, Water, Paper

Michael McKernan, *Here Is Their Spirit: A history of the Australian War Memorial*, University of Queensland Press and the Australian War Memorial, 1991.

What Did You Do in the War, Sandy?

Barry Humphries and Collin O'Brien, *The Life and Death of Sandy Stone*, Pan Macmillan, 1990.

Barry Humphries, *More Please: An autobiography*, Viking, 1992.

K.S. Inglis, "Letters from a Pilgrimage", *Inside Story*, 24 April 2015.

From a Distance

Carolyn Holbrook, "Making Sense of the Great War Centenary", in Carolyn Holbrook and Keir Reeves (eds), *The Great War: Aftermath and commemoration*, University of New South Wales Press, 2019.

Arthur Stace's Single Mighty Word

Keith Dunstan, *Ratbags*, Sun Books, 1979.

Roy Williams with Elizabeth Meyers, *Mr Eternity: The story of Arthur Stace*, Acorn Press & the Bible Society, 2017.

Afternoon Tea with Mary Gilmore

Sylvia Lawson, *Mary Gilmore*, Oxford University Press, 1967.

W.H. Wilde, *Courage a Grace: A biography of Mary Gilmore*, Melbourne University Press, 1988.

W.H. Wilde & T. Inglis Moore, *Letters of Mary Gilmore*, Melbourne University Press, 1980.

Lifting the Shadow

Alison Alexander, *Tasmania's Convicts: How felons built a free society*, Allen & Unwin, 2010.

Mark Baker, *Phillip Schuler: The remarkable life of one of Australia's greatest war correspondents*, Allen & Unwin, 2016.

Roy Bridges, *That Yesterday Was Home*, Australasian Publishing Company, 1948.

You're Not Going to Buy It, Are You?

Frank Bongiorno, *The Eighties: The decade that transformed Australia*, Black Inc., 2015.

Liz Conor, "Friday essay: the politics of Aboriginal kitsch", *The Conversation*, 3 March 2017.

Inga Clendinnen, *Dancing with Strangers*, Text Publishing, 2003.

Charles Darwin, George Frankland and Me

E.T. Emmett, *Tasmania by Road and Track*, Melbourne University Press, 1952.

F.W. & J.M. Nicholas, *Charles Darwin in Australia*, Cambridge University Press, 1989.

Amy Rowntree, *Battery Point Today and Yesterday*, Education Department, Tasmania, 1951.

Michael Sharland, *Stones of a Century*, Oldham, Beddome & Meredith, 1952.

A Rainy Day in Hobart

Jason Byrne et. al, "Lessons in resilience: What city planners can learn from Hobart's floods", *The Conversation*, 18 May 2018.

Ben Chifley's Pipe

Colleen Burke, *Doherty's Corner: The life and work of Marie E.J. Pitt*, Angus & Robertson, 1985.

Michelle Grattan (ed.), *Australian Prime Ministers*, New Holland, 2010.

Jillian Koshin, *Electric Eric: The life and times of Eric Reece, an Australian state premier*, Bokprint, 2009.

Henry Reynolds, *A History of Tasmania*, Cambridge University Press, 2012.

John Curtin's Potato

Michelle Grattan (ed.), *Australian Prime Ministers*, New Holland, 2010.

Eileen Power, *Medieval People*, Methuen, 1924.

Previously published material reproduced with permission

Lines from "Such Silence" by Mary Oliver first published in *Blue Horses* in 2024. Reprinted by the permission of The Charlotte Sheedy Literary Agency as agent for the author. Copyright © 2014 by Mary Oliver with permission of Bill Reichblum

Douglas Stewart's "Arthur Stace's Single Mighty Word", originally published in *Selected Poems*, Angus & Robertson, 1973. Lines used by courtesy of The Estate of Douglas Stewart care of Curtis Brown (Australia) Pty Ltd.

Lines from "The Bin Men Go On Strike" by Raymond Queneau translated by Rachel Galvin are reprinted in "You're Not Going to Buy It ... " by the permission of Carcanet Press, Main Library, The University of Manchester, Oxford Road, Manchester.

Lines from the poem "The Names Inlaid" by Geoff Page, originally included in his *Smalltown Memorials*, University of Queensland Press 1975, reprinted by the permission of the author.

The author and publisher of this book welcome any approaches from owners of copyrighted material reproduced in this book. All reasonable efforts were made to gain permission, but in some cases could not be completed.

Acknowledgements

I am deeply grateful to Terri-ann White of Upswell and Peter Browne, editor of *Inside Story*, for their support and belief in my writing.

All historians are indebted to the libraries, archives and museums that hold the original material we need for our research. In this regard I offer thanks to staff at the Australian War Memorial, Libraries Tasmania, the National Archives of Australia, the National Library of Australia and the State Library of Victoria.

Many friends and colleagues – too many to name – have read and commented on the essays in this book. My chums in our little feminist book club already know, I hope, how much I treasure their friendship. I do reserve special mention for Michael Piggott and Christopher Cole who, each in their way, took a deep interest in this project and understood even before I did what I was trying to do.

My sons Harry Sherratt and Eddie Condé celebrated each joyous moment with me as if it was their own.

About Upswell

Upswell Publishing was established in 2021 by Terri-ann White as a not-for-profit press. A perceived gap in the market for distinctive literary works in fiction, poetry and narrative non-fiction was the motivation. In her years as a bookseller, writer and then publisher, Terri-ann has maintained a watch on literary books and the way they insinuate themselves into a cultural space and are then located within our literary and cultural inheritance. She is interested in making books to last: books with the potential to still be noticed, and noted, after decades and thus be ripe to influence new literary histories.

About this typeface

Book designer Becky Chilcott chose Foundry Origin not only as a strong, carefully considered, and dependable typeface, but also to honour her late friend and mentor, type designer Freda Sack, who oversaw the project. Designed by Freda's long-standing colleague, Stuart de Rozario, much like Upswell Publishing, Foundry Origin was created out of the desire to say something new.

www.ingramcontent.com/pod-product-compliance
Lightning Source LLC
Chambersburg PA
CBHW030654230426
43665CB00011B/1094